Sarada Ranganathan Endowment for Library Science Series. 3

DOCUMENTATION

GENESIS AND DEVELOPMENT

Documentation
Genesis and Development

S R Ranganathan
National Research Professor in Library Science and
Honorary Professor,
Documentation, Research and Training Centre,
Bangalore

Ess Ess Publications
4837/24, Ansari Road
Darya Ganj
New Delhi-110 002
Phone: 51563444
Fax: 51563334
E-mail: info@essessreference.com
url: http://www.essessreference.com

Shiyali Ramamritam **Ranganathan** (1892-1972)

Edition 1 1973
Reprinted 2006

ISBN: 81-7000-476-4

2;5*2
N73

Rs.500/-

Published By:
Ess Ess Publications
4837/24, Ansari Road,
Darya Ganj,
New Delhi-110 002
Ph.No. 23260807, 51563444, Fax: 51563334
E-mail: info@essessreference.com
url: www.essessreference.com

For:

Sarada Ranganathan Endowment for Library Science
702, 'Upstairs',
42nd Cross, III Block,
Rajajinagar,
Bangalore-560 010.
Ph.No. 23305109
E-mail: srels@vsnl.com

Printed in India at: Printline, New Delhi

CONTENTS

SARADA RANGANATHAN LECTURES

1 From Little Acorns, by B I Palmer. 1965

2 United Nations Family of Libraries, by P K Garde. 1966

3 Sociological Foundations of Librarianship, by J H Shera. 1967

4 Library Classification: Evolution of a Dynamic Theory, by R S Parkhi. 1968

5 Teaching of Library Classification, by D W Langridge. 1969

6 Putting Knowledge to Work: An American View of the Five Laws of Library Science, by Pauline Atherton. 1970

7 Reference Service: The Penultimate Purpose of Library Work, by Dr (Mrs) Susheela Kumar. 1971

THE FIVE LAWS OF LIBRARY SCIENCE

1 Books are for use

2 Every reader his/her book

3 Every book its reader

4 Save the time of the reader

5 A library is a growing organism

CHAPTER a

CONSPECTUS

1 Talk to Indian Documentalists

11 Invitation to give the Talk

This book arose out of a talk to a large number of young librarians. As a result of my old age forcing me to give up my usual frequent professional travel to places outside Bangalore, I had no chance during the last six years to meet my colleagues, especially the newcomers into the profession. I was unhappy about it. But a chance came in November 1970 to have my urge satisfied to some extent. For, Shri Ajit Mukherjee, Vice-President of the Iaslic, and Shri Phani Bhushan Roy, its Secretary, told me that about 200 documentalist-librarians had come to Bangalore to attend the Sixth All India Seminar of the Iaslic (1970) and that they would like to hear me or at least to meet me. My house being too small to entertain an audience of 200 persons, I agreed to address them in DRTC (Documentation Research and Training Centre). Though getting out of the house had been difficult for about six months, I exercised some strong will and with the help of some friends, I managed to walk across to DRTC. I was delighted to see many brilliant young faces assembled in the hall. At least a hundred of them were new faces to me. I had been booked only for a half-hour talk. But, the fascination of speaking to so many young people made me get out of my frail body, as it were. My talk to the audience was prolonged to about two hours.

12 Conversational Style

The subject of the talk was "Documentation and Kurma-Avatara." The subject was developed in a conversational style. In a few minutes a good rapport was established between the audience and myself. The jubilant mood of the audience induced a similar mood in me. This made me feel as if I were talking to a few friends. Now and again I put questions to the audience and there was always a good response. The talk was taperecorded. A type-script of it was made and sent to the Secretary of the Iaslic for being edited, whetted, and published in one of their media, without changing the conversational style of the talk, though it would occupy more space in print than the normal expository written style.

13 Mixed Style of Exposition in the Book

By the end of 1971 it struck me that it would give me a chance for clarifying my ideas on documentation if I could add a few chapters and make the book more satisfactory to me than publishing the mere talk. I felt that the exposition of the newly added chapters should not be in the conversational style, but should be in a serious prose style. At the same time I did not wish to spoil the first half of the book by changing its conversational style as it would bring the readers into greater intimacy with me. This accounts for the mixed style of exposition in this book.

2 Conspectus vs Abstract

Chap c forms a Conspectus of the whole book, in the ancient Indian tradition coming down from the *Ramayana*, the work of Valmiki, the earliest known poet of our land. The conspectus forms part of the book. It is not merely an abstract prefixed to the text after the fashion brought out by the West about a century ago in regard to papers published in periodicals.

2 Reciprocity between Documentation and Research

Chap d brings out the reciprocity involved in the work

of a documentalist, and of a research worker and of a policy maker in a Government. It also gives an anecdote showing the reluctance of governmental people to accept a documentalist as a partner in their work.

4 Defined Technical Terminology

Chap e to g emphasise the need for defined terminology in any book or paper. The danger of its absence is illustrated by the confusion caused by not giving the definition of the term 'Document' as part of technical terminology. Chap g shows the generic nature of the term 'documentation' to denote documentation work — the work of cataloguing with emphasis on microdocuments and specialist readers — and Reference service with emphasis on service of nascent microdocuments and specialist readers — often denoted by the alternative term 'Documentation Service' to emphasise this new field of reference service. The same chapter points out that reprograph service and translation service do not belong to the umbral region of documentation, but are only fringe disciplines within the province of technicians and translators. Chap h describes the five stages in the evolution of reference service and equates documentation service with long-range reference service forming stage 4.

Chap j and k explain the 'Why' of documentation, from the angle of social necessity and of growth of technological research respectively.

5 Analogy of Churning the Milky Ocean

Chap m describes the universe of subjects as the analogue of the Milky Ocean and documentation as the analogue of the churn in the puranic episode about the Churning of the Milky Ocean.

6 Agency for Reference Service and of its Place in Library Work

Chap n refers to the historical seizing of documentation

by scientists themselves and its being handed over slowly though reluctantly to the library profession. Chap p shows with the help of a diagram that reference service is the *Summum bonum* of library work, the Five Laws of Library Science being the foundation.

Chap q shows with the help of a diagram that reference service is the hub of all other items of library work.

7 'How' of Documentation

Chap r to t explain the 'How' of documentation and give several analogies and illustrations from Indian classics.

8 Salary and Status of Library Profession

Chap u to z are turned on the salary and the status of the library profession of which documentation is a wing in Departments of Governments, in research institutions, in universities, in colleges, and in public libraries.

9 National and International Documentation Centres

The contents page shows in a fairly significant way the topics covered in regard to the agencies for documentation — international and national — and the division of labour among them. Chap K on "Indian National Social Science Documentation Centre" is elaborately developed so as to be of help to the Insodoc as well as to other national documentation centres of that type. Chap M elaborates the right functions of the Iaslic.

CHAPTER b

ADDRESS TO THE IASLIC MEMBERS

1 The Young and the Old

It has been very kind of you to have come all the way to DRTC and, as Ajit Mukherjee said, "walking on feet to digest your food" (Laughter). I am the greatest beneficiary by your all coming here in such large numbers, because as my friends will tell you, how my health improves in the midst of young librarians. I am quite sure that when I go back home after an hour among you, allowed for me — not for me alone, but for me and for you to put questions — I am quite sure that my wife will not be able to recognise me in my youthful condition (Laughter). But you have come here at your peril, because you are going to listen to an old old garrulous fellow. But, forgetting that everybody will be anxious to have the tea that is awaiting you at the other end, Ajit has asked me to go on in full measure. Well, that is your first peril. The second peril is that you are going to listen to an old man with old views. You are all young people; it is very difficult for young people to tolerate the old views of old people. But we old people too have to tolerate the young people's views. Otherwise, we will not be able to exist! (Laughter)

2 Value of the Essentials of Our Culture

Actually, the very subject of my address, if you had known about it, I am sure many of you would not have come here. They have not announced it; is it not? (Ajit says, "No"). It has been very clever on their part. For, they know that if they had announced it, I would have had only a dozen of your older organisers as my audience (Laughter). They too would have been present mostly out of courtesy. The subject of my talk belongs to the old puranas. I do not think that the young men here have known the puranas, except to dislike them! (Laughter). I am an old puranic man. 'Purana' means 'Old'. Is it not so? I have benefited a good deal from our old culture. It does not mean that I have accepted everything in our old culture.

3 Don't Throw Away the Baby with the Bath Water

At the same time, it does not mean that I throw away everything in our culture. As the saying goes, I do not throw the baby away with the bath water, as some young people do. Somehow I have been helped by great souls to select what is of permanent value in our culture, and to respect, and to live them, and to give up only those out of tune with our times. Now my subject is puranic, I told you.

4 Comprehension of Old and New Concepts

My subject comprehends modern and ancient concepts. It is Documentation — the latest subject in Library Science — and Kurma-Avatara — a puranic subject. I do not think that you may like this combination. In spite of it, "Documentation and Kurma-Avatara"; that is what I propose to talk about.

CHAPTER c

INDIAN TRADITION OF CONSPECTUS

1 My Method of Presentation

My method of presentation will be according to the tradition in our culture. In our tradition, whether it is a book or an article or a speech — if a book the first chapter, if a paper the first paragraph, and if a speech its beginning — generally gives the gist of the whole book or of the whole paper or of the whole speech.

2 Valmiki's Ramayana as an Example

Let me see how many of you have heard of Valmiki's *Ramayana?* Oh so many of you! How many of you have read the *Valmiki-Ramayana?* Very good, so many even in 1970! The *Ramayana* is an excellent example of how a text is begun, in Indian tradition.

3 First Chapter : A Conspectus of the Whole Epic

The very first chapter of the *Ramayana* is a model for us to emulate. This single chapter at the beginning gives the essence of the whole *Ramayana* consisting of hundreds of chapters. In fact, the name that is given to the first chapter is extremely modern. In Sanskrit it is called "*Samkshepa-Ramayana*". In English, it means the "Conspectus (or Synopsis) of Ramayana."

4 Modern Idea of Abstract only a Century Old

Don't you know the accepted standard is that every paper should have an abstract prefixed to the text? I was just checking up with Professor Neelameghan today, as to when the idea of giving an abstract of a paper at its very beginning came into vogue. I think it came into vogue some time in the latter part of the nineteenth century.

Before that, they had not thought of prefixing an abstract to a paper, or a conspectus to a book.

5 The Conspectus of my Book is a part of it

I am sure that you have all eaten the seed of a cashewnut. Have you seen the fruit of cashewnut? What is the peculiarity of the cashewnut? (A Voice.— The seed is not inside the fruit; it is somewhere outside it). The abstract of a paper is outside the text, like the cashewnut (Laughter). On the other hand, the conspectus of a book falls within it, as Chapter 1. Valmiki had set the example in this matter. But I have to be a modern man. Otherwise, nobody will accept me. I want to be accepted by you (Laughter). So in my papers, I put the abstract outside the paper. But in my books, I do not. I call the very first chapter of my book 'Conspectus'. Nowadays, I do not call it "Introduction", "Preface" or any such thing. This is what I have done in this book also, whose text begins only hereafter. Till now, I had been trying only to come to an understanding with you. Therefore, the chapters a to c, are only pre-conspectus chapters.

CHAPTER d

DOCUMENTALIST, RESEARCH WORKER, AND BUSINESS MAN

1 Productivity

I shall begin with the *"Samkshepa Ramayana"*. As I have to keep a large audience in good humour with some interest in the talk, my Conspectus has to be padded considerably, and thus elongated. But I am sure that you will see how short it could have been made, otherwise. According to me, documentation is a necessity today. For what reason? It is necessary in order to ensure adequate productivity in industry. Without documentation, productivity cannot be what it should be. You know what productivity is: output divided by input. It must be as great as possible. If there is any mathematician among the audience here, he may say, "we will make the output 'infinity' by making the input 'zero'" (Laughter). This should not be. You must put in your best and get the best out of it.

2 Documentation: A Necessity

If we are going to get the best out of our industries, documentation is an absolute necessity. Secondly, even before the industries came, we were having research. Without documentation, research too cannot be as productive as it should be. In other words, the research potential cannot be conserved absolutely. We want documentation to come in — that is the library profession to come in. What is the status of the library profession in this? Not as somebody's under-dog, but as an equal partner with those engaged in research. "Without me, no research," we shall say. To that they will say, "Without research, no documentation". Yes, reciprocity. This is not easily understood. Even today, it is not easily granted by all. But surely, scholars are slowly beginning to realise this mutual relation.

3 Documentation and the Business of Government

Even governmental business cannot be conducted in the most efficient way, to the greatest benefit of all the people, if Government's administration continues to be done on the basis of precedents and old files. On the other hand, if Government wants to do its best to its people — the Government must give us what we need, otherwise we can send them out — they must necessarily make use of the services of a documentalist. "How?", the governmental people may ask. We may not ask this question, because we are all documentalists.

4 Hyderabad Cabinet Anecdote

I shall tell you how I was put this question by a Government Officer. In 1954, I was invited to address the Hyderabad Library Conference. To my surprise my friend Shri Ujlamkar had brought all the members of the Cabinet to the Conference. Therefore my talk was turned on a Government's need for documentation.

5 Ministers' Anxiety to Convert the Civil Servants

After my talk, the Chief Minister and the Education Minister invited me to spend that evening with them.

Minister.— We are Ministers in a democracy; but the rulers are the Bureaucracy! (Laughter). We have to convert our civil servants. You may kindly come and give a talk to them.

SRR.— I am not sure whether a mere talk will be of much use.

Ministers.—We do want you to give a talk.

SRR.— Then early in the morning, please send me two or three stenographers. I shall dictate a Memorandum on how the documentalist should play a vital part in the administration of the Government.

I dictated the notes and asked the Chief Minister to

mimeograph the Memorandum and distribute copies among the Secretaries of the Government and the Members of the Cabinet.

6 Unofficial Cabinet Meeting

The Chief Minister telephoned to me two hours later.

Chief Minister.— I have gone through your Memorandum. It is very good. But, how am I to convince my Bureaucracy? I shall arrange for a Cabinet meeting at 4.00 — an unofficial Cabinet Meeting — to which all the Secretaries of the Government will be invited. Please come and spare an hour.

SRR.— I have an engagement and I have to go away at 5.00. You should therefore relieve me in good time for it.

As soon as I went to the meeting, the haughty bureaucracy was contemptuous of me. They looked as if they asked though in silence,"What is the matter? The Cabinet has asked a mere librarian to come and address this meeting and asked us, the experienced Secretaries, to listen to it?" (Laughter). Obviously they were resenting it.

7 Relaxation Room Episode

As soon as I went in, instead of allowing the Chief Minister to take up the subject arranged for the meeting, one of the Secretaries began to talk.

Secretary.— Sir, we have got a small room outside; we want to fit it up as our relaxation room. Shall we decide it first? We have asked the Engineer also to come here for this purpose. We want the room to be fitted for relaxation and recreation, such as playing cards.

SRR — Can this not be discussed after I go away? This does not require any documentation. I have to go out at 5.00.

Chief Minister.— A car was waiting for him even when I came in.

SRR.—Gentlemen, you have had a copy of my Memorandum with you. If you have any questions, plase ask?

One after another.—You tell us something.

SRR.—It is to avoid a long talk from me on documentation in Government Departments — from A to Z — that I sent you my Memorandum in advance.

(They looked at one another).

8 Gist of my Memorandum

Chief Secretary, a fine man, not a sun-dried ICS (Pre-Gandhian Indian Civil Service man) but an IAS (Post-Gandhian Indian Administrative Service man).—Sir, I make the confession on behalf of my colleagues here. We have not read the Memorandum (Laughter).

Chief Minister.—What can I do? Can you kindly tell them the gist of your Memorandum?

SRR.—Hereafter in free India, Administration cannot go on merely on the basis of precedents and files. On the other hand, it must be properly aerated with the latest thought in administrative methods, with the latest theory that has been developed, with the latest practices that have been introduced in other countries. Unless you know all of them you cannot run the administration efficiently to the advantage of the people. Therefore, whenever any resolution comes up before your Cabinet or your Legislature, whenever a Bill comes before the Legislature or whenever your Cabinet wants to make any serious decision, I have recommended in this Memorandum that the Secretary concerned should send a copy of it confidentially to the Librarian. I may say on behalf of my profession, that you may rest assured that he will keep it strictly confidential. He will not tell anybody about it. Then your librarian will collect all the information about the latest developments on it — theory as well as practice — and then give a digest of them to the Secretary or to the Minister himself, if he desires it. On the basis of the information thus furnished, you make your decision.

91 An I C S Secretary Deflated

Among the Secretaries there was only one I C S man.

ICS Man.—So, you want your librarian to be a Super-Secretary?

SRR.—Certainly not, my dear friend. Do not get afraid of it. He will be your equal and not a super-secretary.

How can he swallow it?

92 Will Government Secretaries learn the value of documentation?

Therefore I say, although Professor Neelameghan thinks he has brought down some of the industries to accept documentation and some of the universities where research is going on to accept documentation, I do not know if he has ever attempted any Government to accept it (Laughter). Whether he will succeed or at least his successor will succeed, I do not know (Renewed laughter). However, I remember one fortunate case. One of the senior officers of the Home Ministry of the Government of India came to DRTC along with his librarian and asked for advice about the organisation of Documentation for his Ministry. This was a voluntary request. They spent about a week with me and got some ideas. However, I learnt later that the Government refused his request to sanction the post of a Documentalist on a higher scale of salary than the current one as documentation requires a person with a higher intellectual ability.

CHAPTER e

TECHNICAL TERMINOLOGY

1 Ancient Practice

According to Indian tradition, after the Conspectus we have a chapter on Terminology (*Pari-bhasha*). The terminology chapter usually begins with Undefined or Assumed Terms, and gradually builds up the defined technical terms used in the text. This is an excellent practice to prevent refracton of ideas in the minds of readers.

2 Absence of Homonyms and Synonyms

The Technical Terminology avoids homonyms and synonyms. This prevents any possible distraction of the readers, while reading the text. Unfortunately, in the modern writings on our subject, this wholesome practice is not followed.

SRR.— Can you tell me two different senses in which the term 'Order' is used by many writers on library science? (Silence for a few minutes). Can nobody recall the different meanings?

A Voice.—"Sequence", is one meaning.

Another Voice.— "The degree of remove of a sub-class from the original class", is another meaning.

SRR.— Very good.

A third voice.— They use the word 'term' to denote either the "name of an idea" or the "number respresenting the idea". This is confusing.

S R R.— Excellent. We must avoid all such homonyms and synonyms. This is something which several writers in our subject have yet to learn.

3 My Practice

I follow our good tradition. I generally put at the very

beginning in a book or in a paper, a chapter or a section on Terminology. Here, I introduce technical terms and define them carefully. I also avoid homonyms and synonyms among them. This is not liked by many librarians.

4 Allergy in Some Librarians

Unfortunately, some librarians are allergic to technical terminology. They even express contempt for it. In reviewing one of my books, a librarian referred to my precisely defined terminology as "Abracadabra". He does not evidently know that most scientific treatises use only defined technical terminology. According to another librarian, I make my books unreadable by the use of defined technical terminology. He wants that common words should be used. He claims that the undertones and overtones of a common word have a charm of their own. He says that the words in a piece of "good writing" should have such undertones and overtones. He does realise how much these will prevent the correct communication of ideas.

SRR.—I should like to know how many of you agree with me. Nobody? Those who agree with me, please hands up. Ajit, please count.

Ajit.—It is quite a large number.

SRR.—Politicians indulge in using common words with overtones and undertones. They do so deliberately. For, they do not want to be precise, so that they can explain away their words, if they land themselves later in a difficult position. I ask you: Are librarians to write and talk like politicians?

Voices.—No, no. We are scientists and not politicians. We must have precise terminology.

SRR.—I am glad that you, the younger generation of librarians, have begun to value the use of defined technical terminology.

5 Shera's Testimony

I remember one experience. In 1964, I was conducting a Seminar on "Colon Classification" at the Rutgers University in the United States. During that Seminar, Dr Jesse H Shera said, "Our people complain that Ranganathan uses pedantic language. He never does it. He defines every word he uses and we have to cooperate with him and understand the words correctly". Mr Bennett (an American librarian attending my speech) knows what a sharp tongue Dr Shera has. Shera continued, "If the American librarians are going to feed themselves only with the *Library journal,* woe unto the library profession!"

CHAPTER f

HAVOC BY AN UNDEFINED TECHNICAL TERM 'DOCUMENT'

1 Indian Standards Institution

The following account of the fate of the first proposal to have a National Documentation Centre in India illustrates the risk of not using or understanding defined technical terms. In 1947, immediately after our Independence, our Government appointed a Standards Body — the I S I (Indian Standards Institution). Dr Lal Verman was appointed as its first Director. He was not sure where to begin. He came to me one day.

Lal Verman.—We have appointed an Executive Committee. We want some Committee which will take up some kind of Standard. Can you form a Committee for your subject?

SRR.—With great pleasure. Whoever is going to ask us Librarians like that!

2 Documentation Committee

Our Committee was the first in the Indian Standards Institution. We called it Documentation Committee. There was no superior body to which it could be attached. So even today, the Documentation Committee is directly attached to the Executive Committee.

3 Promotion of Indian Documentation Centre

31 Stimulus from International Bodies

In 1946, the I S O (International Standards Organisation) became the successor to the pre-war I S A (International Standards Association). This was the result of the action of the United Nations Standards Coordinating Committee. In November 1946, the I S O was requested by the F I D (= International Federation for Documentation) to stimulate the formation of a national documentation committee in each country. On 22 May 1947, the I S O sent a communication on this point to the I S I. About the same time, the F I D wrote to me a letter on the same subject.

32 Action by the Indian Standards Institution

The I S I referred to its Documentation Committee the communication from the I S O. As Chairman, I prepared a memorandum for consideration by the Documentation Committee. It suggested

1 Formation of an Indian National Documentation Committee;

2 Sponsoring of the same by the I S I in the first instance; and

3 Its ultimate relation with a library of national status.

The Documentation Committee of I S I approved this Memorandum. On 29 October 1947, this memorandum was communicated to the Ministry of Education of the Government of India by the I S I. It also expressed its willingness to be the sponsor of the proposed National Documentation Committee, in the first instance.

As usual the Ministry of Education appointed a Committee to consider the proposal.

4 'Document' Mistaken for a 'Historical Document'

One of the members of the Committee was a very good friend of mine. At that time, he was the Director of Archives and Secretary of the Historical Records Commission. He wrote a slashing note, against my proposal.

Archivist.—All documents are looked after by the Historial Records Commission. What business has the library profession to come in here?

I too gave a slash back.

SRR.—Documentation deals not only with historical documents, but also mathematical documents, physics documents, engineering documents, etc. Is the Historical Records Commission competent to deal with all these documents?

Naturally there was no reply. There was thus a stalemate. The Government was on the other side, because it did not ask for any action or expenditure (Laughter). It did not allow anything to move forward. That was all over. The subject had to be started again as described in See J12 to J23.

5 Similar Experience at the International Level

Within a few months thereafter, at the invitation of the F I D (= International Federation for Documentation), I went to The Hague. When I went there, the then President of the F I D was Le Meistre. It was the first time that we met. The first question he put to me was this.

Le Meistre.—Is documentation accepted in your country?

What could I say? I did not say anything, because I did not want to tell an untruth, nor to make an absurd confession about our country. So I was hesitant.

Le Meistre.—I ask you this question, because people are questioning the competence of the F I D to do documentation work. The archivists of a few countries have sent us protest letters.

This made me feel that I was in good company. And then I let the cat out of the bag. I told him all that I have described a few minutes ago, and added that I had written a strong Minute against the contention of our own Archivist.

Le Meistre.—Have you got a copy of the Minute?

SRR.—Yes. I have it in my bag.

He took it from me and had it published in several media in Europe. Such has been the struggle of our profession, even as late as 1948, in spite of its being backed by an international organisation, half a century old.

6 Trouble Due to Not Defining the Term 'Document'

We must be very cautious. We must define the term 'Documentation' carefully. The confusion, as you saw, came out of the term 'Document'. The term 'Document' was brought into its current use in our profession by the French in the 1930's.

7 Definition of 'Document'

What is a document? A document is a graphic record of some idea or some phenomenon, made in words or in pictures. A document can be one of four kinds:—

1 Micro document.—A book of normal size, dealing with a large expanse of subject, or a volume of a periodical;

2 Micro document.—A document such as a paper in a periodical or its reprint, or a short extract from a book, usually dealing with a subject of small extension but of deep intension;

3 Neo document.—This has come into existence during the last few decades.

SRR.—A paper by my friend Ganesh Bhattachahyya for your Iaslic Seminar refers to this. I hope you have seen the volume of papers. Have any of you read the titles of the papers at least? (Turning to Ajit). Probably they could not find time for it (Laughter), because you had so often to eat and so much to travel within the City. How can you find time to read even the titles of the papers expected to be considered at the Conference! (Laughter). Ganesh has dealt in his paper with Standards Specifications, Plans, Data, etc. They are less than micro documents. He calls them "Ultra-micro documents". I call them "Neo documents."

4 Meta document.—A document produced by an instrument, giving a picture of either a natural or social phenomenon, totally unmediated by the human brain.

SRR.—Have any of you seen such a document? Can anybody here tell me an example of a Meta document? Nobody?

A Voice.—Aurora.

SRR.—"Aurora" is a phenomenon. It is not a document. But the photograph of Aurora is a document. Do you mean that?

Voice.—Yes, Sir.

SRR.—I am happy to know that you are aware of such Meta documents. Have any one of you seen a Meta document of a social phenomenon? I don't think so.

The last two kinds also belong to the category of Micro documents.

CHAPTER 9

WHAT OF DOCUMENTATION

1 Two Specialised Activities

What is documentation? The term 'Documentation' is a generic term used to denote two activities:

11 DOCUMENTATION WORK

It corresponds to our old cataloguing work. Nowadays, on account of the present day importance of research, when we say documentation list, we distinguish it from the term 'Bibliographical list' previously in use. A Bibliography is a catalogue of more of whole books than of papers. But, a documentation list places emphasis on micro documents — particularly on nascent micro documents — and on specialist readers. That is a documentation list. Preparing a documentation list is part of documentation. The list may consist merely of entries describing the documents or to each entry may be appended either an annotation or an abstract. The abstract may be merely indicative or informative.

12 DOCUMENTATION SERVICE

In its restricted sense it is a new term used to denote reference service, when the emphasis is on service of micro documents — particularly of nascent micro documents — and on specialist readers. Thus, documentation service is only reference service of an intensive nature. Reciprocally, reference service may be taken to be only documentation service of a less intensive nature. To avoid multiplication of terms, we shall hereafter use the term 'Documentation Service' only, in the general sense of Reference Service, leaving it to be inferred, from the context, whether it is used in the restricted sense or in the unrestriced sense. These are the two and only two parts of Documentation.

2 Reprography Mistaken for Documentation Work

Unfortunately, before we established ourselves as documentalists we were carried off our feet. Photographers come, microfilm makers come, reprographers come. And each of them say, "Documentation is reprography" etc. Persons producing reprographs call themselves Documentalists. Certainly I know of one such person confusing the mind of research organisations. Even some librarians accept this claim of such technicians. When they sit on Selection Committees, they recommend a reprographer to the post of a documentalist. They even regard training in reprography as a necessary part of a course for documentalists. Is it not the job of the technician to take photographs of macro or micro sizes? But, among some persons calling themselves as documentalists, there appears to be a joy in doing some work which is not theirs! I always tell them, "You appoint a technician and ask him to make reprographs. In this work, the role of a documentalist is only to do liaison work between the technician and the reader. If a reader wants a particular document to be owned by him, either in this size or that size, we call the technician and ask him to produce it, and then given it to the reader. That is all a documentalist has to do in reprography. If you become a technician in reprography you cease to be a documentalist. You cannot find time or competence to do both the technician's work and the documentalist's work in full satisfaction."

3 Translation Mistaken for Documentation Work

Another factor of which some documentalists are overfond is the supply of translations. No doubt they should do so. But they believe that they themselves should do the translation to readers. And they even say, "A librarian should know many languages. He should be able to translate documents on any subject from any language into any other language." I am putting it in a rather exaggerated form.

4 Indian Institute of Science : A Concrete Example

In the year 1924, when I myself became the first librarian of the University of Madras, there was an advertisement for the librarian's post in the Indian Institute of Science, Bangalore. They advertised, "Wanted a librarian, for the Indian Institute of Science. Knowledge of at least four European languages is essential. Some knowledge of library technique is desirable" (Laughter). And one of my former colleagues in the Presidency College, Madras, was an Assistant Professor of several languages — Latin, German, French etc. He applied and he got selected. After he joined his new post, he found that very few people wanted translation, because there was very little work done. One day, he came all the way to Madras and asked me, "Can you give me one smart young librarian to come and help me?" Such was the idea in those days.

5 Persistence of Wrong Notion

Unfortunately, a wrong notion persists tenaciously, even as a wrong tradition does. Nowadays, some librarians ask while interviewing candidates, "How many languages do you know?" I do not want to quarrel with the members before the candidates. After the candidates go away, I ask them.

SRR.—Why do you want him to know so many languages?

A Member.—To do translation.

SRR.—Has he not got enough work to do in the library? If a translation is wanted, appoint a translator.

6 Fringe of Documentation Work

Reprography and translation, I call "Fringes" of our field of work. Here we have to do only liaison work, not the actual work. I do not know how many of you agree with this. I want to know how the young generation of librarians think about it. How many of you would like to become documentalists in the sense of a photographer? Anybody? Nobody! Don't be shy if you feel like that.

Turning to the Chairman, "I hope they are all speaking the truth."

How many of you would like to become translators in the name of a documentalist? Nobody? Are you sure? Well, keep to that resolution. Remember that there is a dangerous fascination in man to do and to talk about other people's work and neglect his own legitimate work. Beware of this dangerous fascination. It is like the fascination of the precipice!

7 A Question from the Audience

A Voice.—How can one do documentation service without knowing several languages?

SRR.—How many languages are you going to learn to provide documentation service?

A Voice.—What do your mean by several languages?

SRR.—There is no limit to that.

A Voice.—What is the limit you put?

SRR.—Can you learn all the languages? I put the limit: Know one language well. And then try to learn to "read the backs of books" in some other languages, provided the script is known to you. You know what is meant by "reading the backs" and title pages, and to translate them into your own language. This does not require a course in German, Italian, French, etc. Any librarian who has got a head on his shoulders can learn this in a few days.

8 Securing the Service of a Translator

A Reader.—I want this particular article. Since you have already given the title page, etc, you can read the book. Because you have given a class number, etc, you know what the subject is about. I do not know German. But I want a translation of it. Can you translate it for me?

Librarian.—Please give me some time. I shall get it translated by a gentleman who can translate from German into English.

Reader.—Are there such people?

Librarian.—There are people who can translate from German. I have with me the names of a panel of such persons. But I cannot give it to any of those persons. I must find out from them a person familiar with your subject. Otherwise you can imagine how monstrous the translation would become.

Ajit.—We have paid the penalty for it.

SRR.—Everybody would have paid the penalty for it if he had attempted to do it.

91 Limit to the Documentalist's Knowledge of Language

So, do not think that I am saying, "Shut out languages." I thought that as librarians you would have all known about it. You must know enough to read the title page and then if you have some experience — you cannot learn it in one day, you cannot learn it in the school — if you have been a librarian for some time working under somebody, if you are interested, you can glance through some of these books; then you learn a little more of translation, so that you can pick out points for cross reference, and so on. You need not take a course in German for that. I do not know whether you are satisfied with this answer. If you have any more questions, please ask.... Nothing more? You seem to have some doubt; your face shows it (Laughter). No? I am glad. Do not imagine that you will become a great documentalist by becoming a great translator. No, not at all.

CHAPTER h

STAGES IN THE EVOLUTION OF DOCUMENTATION SERVICE

1 Stage 1 : Primitive Documentation Service

In the earliest stage when there were only a few documents to be served out, and fewer scholars to be served, documentation service merely consisted of picking out and giving to a scholar any document mentioned by him. This may be denoted by the term 'Primitive Documentation Service'. For this primitive form, it was not necessary either to know the contents of the different documents, or to know the field of specialisation or of the standard of the respective readers. An ordinary literate — even an experienced semi-literate — would have proved sufficient.

2 Stage 2 : Ready Reference Service

In 1876, Melvil Dewey, the creator of the modern library profession and the inventor of many of the modern library techniques, interpreted the initionym 'ALA', denoting the American Library Association, to mean "Ask Library Anything." This was indeed a stroke of genius. But, this was first interpreted to imply to give only such information to a reader as could be easily found out from an appropriate Ready Reference Book, such as Calendar, Cyclopaedia, Dictionary, Directory or Year Book. This may be denoted by the term "Ready Reference Service." In this form of documentation service, the documentalist was called Ready Reference Librarian. His range of knowledge could be limited to that of Ready Reference Books. This species of documentation service is still continuing along with the later species and it is but proper that this should continue to be practised.

3 Stage 3 : Floor-Duty

Some decades later, the Public Library System developed the practice of putting one member of the library staff in the stack-room. His duty was to help each reader — most of the readers were only generalist readers — in the choice of the book — a whole book — on the subject of interest to him at the moment. In choosing it, he had to see that its contents, its exposition, and its style of expression, were all within the capacity of the reader. This may be denoted by the term 'Floor-Duty'. In this form, the documentalist was called "Librarian on Floor-Duty." His range of knowledge could be limited to the books of an ordinary kind, without too much of specialisation. A single person was often sufficient to serve all the readers. This species of documentation service is still continuing along with the later species and it is but proper that this should continue to be practised in every generalist library — be it Public or Academic.

4 Stage 4 : Long Range Reference Service: Specialised Documentation Service

When I was studying the working of the British Library System in 1924-25, I saw both Ready Reference Service, and Floor-Duty Work, in full steam in public libraries. But somehow, I felt these to be insufficient. But it was only a vague feeling. One day, this feeling was given a concrete shape, on hearing Prof E C Richardson of USA, about the new system of "Research Consultants" being then introduced in the Library of Congress. In 1928, I began in the Madras University Library, intensive service to specialist readers, who were then very few in number. By 1930, it was developed to a full measure, with the help of five full-time members of the staff assigned to this work. I then called it "Long Range Reference Service." For, it required much more time than Ready Reference Service and a search through quite a long range of micro documents. Today, this species of documentation service is defined as "Service with emphasis on nascent micro-documents and on specialist readers." The term "Specialised Documentation Service" may be used instead of the term "Long Range Reference Service." This fourth species of documentation service is now being valued by all research institutions — academic, industrial, commercial houses — and even by some departments of Governments. Hereafter, this species of documentation service is likely to be given more widely than before. It must be so, in order to meet the social needs of today characterised by high population pressure.

5 Stage 5 : Help Towards Self-Realisation

There is yet another stage to be reached by documentation service. In that stage, documentation service will go beyond serving generalist readers with books for ordinary kind of information and for leisure-time entertainment. It will go beyond serving the generalist readers with literature, biographies, and other works of an elevating kind, capable of sublimating the lower emotions into higher ones. It will also go beyond feeding the intellect of specialists even of the most severe kind. What then will be the purpose of documentation service in Stage 5? The purpose will be to:

1 Make an honest and fair attempt to stimulate intuition;

2 Activate the unexpressed craving for mystic experience and self-realisation; and

3 Release the "Inner-man" so as to transcend the bondage of time and space, and to help the realisation of the "One-ness of all things" in spite of the intellect differentiating all things to the point of atomisation, and thereby help reaching towards a Stage of Bliss.

This kind of documentation service cannot be given to every reader; nor can it be given by every documentalist.

It can be given only by a documentalist that can sense the ripeness of the reader for it. He can be an adept in sensing this, only if he himself has had, at least in certain moments, an experience of the flavour and quality of mystic experience. At the present stage, the number of persons either capable of taking this form of documentation service, or of sensing the readers' capability for receiving it and giving it to them is indeed very few. But, there are at least some readers struggling to pass beyond sensory and intellectual experience, and to get at least momentary glimpses of Holistic experience.

6 India's Responsibility

In the large sociological experiment being conducted by nature through centuries, the West is said to have "burnt the witches." This action appears to have resulted, unintentionally though it might have been, in either the liquidation of persons with self-realisation or in driving them "underground" — leading a life escaping detection. But, as if to serve the purpose of a "control" in the sociological experiment, the self-realised persons of India still continue to be free and even revered. Of late a few persons from the "exhausted" West also seek to have the benefit of spending at least some time in the "Presence" of a self-realised Indian. For example, some of those sought an opportunity to spend some time in the "presence" of Sri Ramana Maharshi of Thiruvannamalai in South India, when I was University Librarian in Madras. I have had first hand account of the "Experience" of some of such visitors from the West.

7 Wish

The few Documentalists needed for the full play of the fifth stage of documentation service will have to come from among these self-realised persons. Their service cannot be hired. They cannot be pressed into service by us intellectuals. They will do their work spontaneously, at the right time, with the right readers. When they do volunteer to do this form of service in a Library they should be accepted with all humility. To say this does not mean that the ordinary members of the library profession have nothing to do with the matter. On the other hand, there is at least something small that they should do. Just as libraries are now acquiring documents for specialists, they should also acquire documents with a mystic flavour. They will be largely in the form of biographies, travel books, sacred books, and poems of unusual mystic origin and quality. But this is not enough. The "Cold printed words" of a document will generally screen away the mystic element. Therefore, the "Cold printed words" of such a document should be dowered with the personality of a documentalist, if they have to reveal the mystic elements even to the readers having some craving for it. This means that there should be among the documentalists, some one, who has just a touch of mystic element in him. His work with the readers should not have even a remote element of compulsion. It is difficult to describe in words anything more. But the documentalists with a touch of mystic element will know how best to give the fifth species of documentation service. Perhaps, India has more opportunity than any other country to give this species of documentation service. My wish is that India should fulfil this duty, in helping humanity to reach a higher level of life.

8 Social Benefit of Stage 5 of Documentation Service

In addition to helping isolated individuals towards their self-realisation, Stage 5 of documentation service will also lead society gradually towards an amicable co-existence — intra-national coexistence as well as inter-national coexistence. At present, it is the lower emotions that create tension and lead to civil war or international war. By the slow expansion and success of Stage 5 of documentation service, these lower emotions will be sublimated into higher emotions, revealing the One-ness of Man in all humanity. It is not claimed that this will happen within a predictable period. All that is meant is that this form of service should be one of the ideals to be remembered and approximated to. The ultimate fulfilment of library service will be in the measure of the degree of approximation to this ideal, though it may be described by some as an Utopian Ideal.

CHAPTER j

'WHY' OF DOCUMENTATION: SOCIAL NECESSITY

1 Social Economy

We now pass on to the 'Why' of documentation. In this Chapter, we use the term 'Documentation Service' as it is in its stage 4 (*See* Sec h4). Yesterday, I got from Professor Neelameghan a copy of the *Indian Express* containing a report of the speech of Dr Mukherjee — the President of Iaslic. Dr Mukherjee has answered the question. He has answered it not as a documentalist, but as a specialist needing documentation service. I hope you remember his words. I need not repeat them. A specialist wants documentation service — and therefore documentation — because the amount of literature produced is so great that he cannot afford to wade through every document — particularly micro document — to find out which is more appropriate to him at the moment. Is it not so? This is a social necessity. It is necessary to secure social economy.

2 Rise in the Standard of Life

Today, for various reasons, our standard of life has gone up enormously. When I was a child, till I went to the University — mind you, here I make a confession — I used to wear only a towel which would begin at the waist and end at the knees. That was all. Perhaps you will now call it "Gandhian apparel." But it was widely prevalent in my younger days. When I visited Ceylon in 1950, I found that even in that late year most University graduates were wearing only Gandhian apparel. You young people cannot believe this. But now, within ten days of his coming into this world, my grandchild had to be given four coats. Nowadays, even a table must be clothed. The dog must have a clothing, and so the horse, and even the cow; is it not so? So, our standard of life — whether you like it or not — has gone up.

3 Democracy and Standard of Life

Secondly, the number of persons who want to come to higher standards of life, is increasing every day. It is going to increase for ever. We are in an age of democracy. You cannot have one standard for that man and quite another for this man. A little bit of arithmetic will show you what the effect of this is on the quality of commodities we must produce. Tremendous. I leave the calculation to you. I guess that we now want a thousand times more of each commodity — whether it is clothes, building, or whatever it is — than what was sufficient about a century ago.

How are you going to get them? You cannot get them unless you supplement natural commodities by artificial ones. Even for food, we have to depend upon artificial commodities.

4 "Meals for Millions"

As Indians, you might have heard of the organisation known as "Meals for Millions". Have you? What about it? The Government of India is running the "Meals for Millions' with its headquarters in Delhi. I had been to that organisation and observed its work. It is now serving throughout India. Actually we have to bring into use raw materials not directly consumable and ask the technologist to make them consumable. If a raw material is poisonous, the technologist should remove the poisonous principle from it and make the material consumable.

5 Burma Bean Anecdote

I remember even now an experience of mine, with a shudder. In 1938-39, I came to Bangalore for some purpose. At that time there were a large number of deaths in some hotels of Tamil Nadu. On investigation the Government discovered that it was due to what was called the "Burma beans." When the Burma beans were examined, a poisonous principle was found in them. So, immediately the Government prohibited the use of Burma beans. When I came to Bangalore there was a biochemist who was a friend of mine. He asked me to have a meal with him in his house. When I went to his house, he gave me a first class dish for eating — I do not know the all-India name for it; in Tamil, we call it "Vadai," a salty circular cake with a hole in the centre. (Ajit .— It is called Vada everywhere). Very good. My host supplied me with vadas; it was very crisp, very tasty, very nice. I ate it even more than I could. I was enjoying it. "Do you like it?" his wife asked me. "Yes," I said. She said, "It is made of Burma beans" (Laughter). I immediately felt that I was dying (Laughter). Then her husband assured me that I would not die and that as a biochemist he had removed all the poisonous principle from the Burma beans.

6 Food Research Laboratory

After our Independence, on account of insufficiency of natural food materials, that very biochemist was chosen by Pandit Nehru to head a Food Technological Laboratory, established in Mysore. Is there any representative of that Institute here? Sangameswaran is here. What about the other officer, Dastur? Sangameswaran may not know this story. Let me tell him. He may go and tell his people about it.

7 Nehru Heckled

Perhaps, it was in the year 1950 that the Food Laboratory was started. There was at that time a Parliamentarian whose business was always to oppose the Government, and particularly to heckle Nehru, because Nehru was a towering personality. He said, "Nehru having taken science in Cambridge in his youger days, is mad after science; he is spending crores of rupees on laboratories, and the latest madness is establishing a Food Technological Laboratory. Can we make food in a laboratory?" (Laughter). That was the question. But, Nehru was too clever for these people. He did not answer this in the Parliament, because he took it to be a question arising out of scepticism and ignorance.

8 Nehru's Reply-in-Action

A few days later, Nehru invited for a Dinner a few Members of the Parliament including that gentleman. The rice was unusually nice. You call it Dehra Dun rice in the North. Is it not so? But this was better than the Dehra Dun rice, for the reason that all the grains were exactly of the same length and exactly of the same thickness. It was a sight to see a heap of rice in which every grain was exactly like every other. They all had a good dinner and then the table was turned against Pandit Nehru again! The Opposition Member asked: "Sir, is such a fine Dehra Dun rice reserved only for the Prime Minister? (Laughter). Why is it not given to us?" Then Nehru said, "This is not Dehra Dun rice. This is rice prepared in Mysore by the Food Research Laboratory." This is a fact. I was in Delhi at that time. I got this information first hand, because one of his Secretaries knew me very well and he told me all this.

9 Other Artificial Commodities

So what I am saying is, that we have now to produce all kinds of artificial commodities. Take building materials as another example. How many houses are being built now? Can you manage with the old natural building materials? What are the building materials now being used? Lime stone, powdered with coarse sand, then some thin steel rods put into it, and the whole thing is called Reinforced concrete. Many buildings are now being built with reinforced concrete. Well, you can easily multiply examples. So it is necessary — it is a social necessity now — that technology should produce consumable commodities out of natural materials not directly consumable. This has become an absolute social necessity. Therefore what are we to do? We have not only to step up research in our own country, but also use the results of research done in other countries.

CHAPTER k

'WHY' OF DOCUMENTATION: GROWTH OF TECHNOLOGICAL RESEARCH

1 Growth in Number of Research Workers

Look at Table 1 given hereunder. You will find in it the number of research personnel in some countries.

Table 1: Estimated Research Man Power in 1962

Country	Research personnel	
	1962	1970
China	2,400,000	
United States	1,160,000	4,000,000
USSR (1967)	770,000	
United Kingdom	211,000	
Germany	142,000	
Japan (1966)	129,000	
France	111,000	
India	80,000	120,000
Netherlands	33,000	
Belgium	22,000	

11 USSR

In 1900 or so, all the research workers of USSR could be seated on one sofa! (Laughter). The salary paid to those research workers was nothing compared to the money spent on the stables of the Czars (Laughter).

But what is happening now? You will find this also in the table. USSR is now spending almost one hundred times more, taking into account all the research workers in all the subjects.

12 China

Take China. The number of research workers has increased four times during the last five years.

13 UNITED STATES OF AMERICA

In 1970, the research workers in USA were four million in number.

14 INDIA AND BELGIUM

In this year — 1970 — the number of research workers in India is one hundred and twenty thousand. In Belgium, it is only thirty thousand. Why? Does this mean that India is more advanced in research than Belgium? Here you must interpret the figures meaningfully. What is the population of India? What is the population of Belgium?

15 OTHER COUNTRIES

We cannot find time now to comment on the data about other countries found in Table 1.

2 Expenditure on Research

Let me next take up the expenditure on research. See Tables 2, 3 and 4 given below.

Table 2: Expenditure on Research in U S A

1930	1947	1953	1964	1970
500	2,000	6,000	50,000	500,000

Table 3: Shift in the Agency Financing Research in U S A

Agency	Before world war II	In 1953	In 1964
University	5%	5%	4%
Industries	60%	40%	32%
Government	35%	55%	64%

In 1930, the expenditure on research in USA was only five hundred million rupees. Now it is five hundred thousand million rupees. Thus within the last 40 years the expenditure on research has increased a thousand times.

Table 4: Sale Proceeds and Research Fund in U S A

SN	Subject	Percentage of sale proceeds set apart for research
1	Instrument and precision products	3.34
2	Electrical machinery and equipment	2.80
3	Printing trade	2.55
4	Miscellaneous	2.25
5	Transport equipment	2.04
6	Chemical products	1.83
7	Non-electrical machinery	1.67
8	Apparel	1.65
9	Fabricated metal products	1.64
10	Rubber products	1.36
11	Food and beverages	1.15
12	Stone and ceramic products	1.11
13	Textile products	0.95
14	Petroleum and coal products	0.74
15	Paper and allied products	0.72
16	Primary metal industry	0.64
17	Lumber and wood products	0.57
18	Furniture and fittings	0.50
19	Leather and its products	0.44

3 Elimination of Time Lag Between a Discovery and Its Application

Another important thing that is happening on account of the social demand is that any discovery made by a man of genius has to be brought into actual use immediately. I now refer to Table 5 given below.

Table 5: Acceleration of Exploitation of New Ideas

SN	Subject	Year of		N of years
		Discovery of principle	Practical application	
1	Photography	1727	1839	112
2	Telephone	1823	1876	53
3	Atomic power release	1932	1945	13
4	Transistor	1940	1948	8
5	Laser	1958	1960	2

It took about 112 years for photography to be brought into wide use after its discovery. Now, Laser discovered only in 1958, is already very much in use. Even children talk about Laser now. You see the quickness with which we are now putting all new ideas into use.

4 Loss Due to Absence of Documentation

What is more significant is the amount of money being wasted by the industry, by the government, and by the research worker, as a result of not having documentation service. Table 6 is devoted to this. See how much money has been lost on account of not having documentation service.

Table 6: Loss in Research Potential

SN	Loss	Field of research	Country
1	Rs 216,000,000	Science in general	UK
2	Rs 15,000,000	Electronics	USA
3	Rs 18,700,000	Electronic translation equipment	USA

5 Shift of Research From Pure to Applied Sciences

Table 7 given below, reveals another modern trend.

Table 7: Major Ideas Created in Different Subjects During Different Periods

Colon Class Number	Main subject	Number of major new ideas and subjects created during the period		
		1451–1700	1701–1900	1901–1950
B	Mathematics	9	24	21
C	Physics	3	21	68
D	Engineering	1	23	46
E	Chemistry	0	36	80
F	Teehnology	0	21	70
G	Biology	2	4	8
H	Geology	1	16	8
I	Botany	1	7	4

Colon Class Number	Main subject	Number of major new ideas and subjects created during the period		
		1451–1700	1701–1900	1901–1950
J	Agriculture	0	2	2
K	Zoology	0	4	4
L	Medicine	4	21	80
	Total	21	180	391

This table shows the shift of emphasis in research from pure to applied sciences. It shows how the modern social well-being depends increasingly on technology and on the research needed for it.

6 Many Implications of the Tables

The data for the tables used in this talk were collected by Prof Neelameghan. After he gave these data to me, a number of ideas began to simmer in my mind—sociological, technological, political, educational, and so on. But I am concerned only with documentation ideas now. Please go through these tables carefully (copies already distributed to the audience).

CHAPTER III

RESEARCH AS CHURN AND DOCUMENTATION AS A STEADYING TOOL

1 Appreciation of Documentation by a Modern Industry: An Example

11 Research in Titanium

I had a personal experience in USA. That was in 1950. In that year, USA had begun to take from our country, the earth found in Kerala, out of which Titanium could be extracted. We did not know the use for it. But they were curious to know it. After finding that something useful can be got out of the ore, they took it away in large ship-loads. When I was in New York, a certain Nickel Company had taken all this Titanium earth. By the time I went there, there were many research workers just experimenting what all commodities could be got out of it. At that time Mrs Lea Bohnert was its Librarian. She belonged to a very distinguished family in Nashville; I had visited her parents. For about 7 or 8 months, she could not find out whether there was any duplication of investigation by the different research workers. It was only in a few cases that she found repetition purely by chance. She felt very worried for not being able to detect duplication of an investigation, before it was started. She was using the DC. In DC, Titanium has got one place. Anything about Titanium will go into that place only. In that library, all the reports were on Titanium. Therefore to each of all the reports, she could give only one DC Number. Is it Classification to give the same number to all the documents? Do you call it Classification? (No, No).

12 Librarian's Enterprise

The librarian felt very vexed. She came to me one day.

Librarian.—Sir, I have been trying to find out some

way of distinguishing these reports, and spreading them out into different classes. I could not do it. I then went to the Columbia University Library. There I found a new Scheme of Classification — Colon Classification (C C). I found your name as its author. Then I went and asked the Library School "Do you know the author of C C?" They said, "Madam, the author is now with us in this University."

That was how she came to me. I was along with one of my friends — S Parthasarathy — who was travelling with me. And she asked me about that scheme.

SRR.—Well, I have not done anything about Titanium. If you bring some of the documents, I may be able to do something.

13 Facet Analysis Gives Relief to Documentation

The librarian brought certain documents. We used our Facet Analysis, and the schedule of isolates. We were able to separate about 20 or 30 reports into different classes. Of course, she was so pleased.

Librarian.—Sir, if I bring some documents every day, will you please do it for me? (Laughter).

SRR.—With great pleasure. I, too can learn something from it.

Parthasarathy and myself, tried to help her. This was going on for some time.

2 The Chief's Appreciation of the Work of the Librarian

21 Chief's Mode of Appreciation

Librarian.—I must tell you a story which I had been hiding from you. After I began to classify the reports, whenever anybody brought a new project, I checked up with my catalogue, and in some cases, I would reject it by saying "So and so has already done it. Here is the report." And the chief found out that he was saving a lot of dollars as a result of this.

As all profit making chiefs do, the Chief sent for his librarian.

Chief.—I find that you are saving a lot of dollars for us.

Librarian.—I am glad to hear it, Sir.

Chief.—Why did you neglect helping us in this way, till now? As a result of your negligence we had already lost a lot of dollars (Laughter).

Librarian.—What can I say, Sir, against this charge? I did not know till now how to classify the reports.

Chief.—How do you know it now?

Librarian.—There is an Indian gentleman from whom I learnt it.

Chief.—You are not taking leave. Why do you go and kill that Indian gentleman that way? You may take leave for this purpose, whenever you want it.

Librarian.—He says that he is very busy in the day time. He is available only in the evenings. So I go in the evenings.

22 Librarian's Anxiety

I must tell you how much value the Chief had begun to attach to Documentation. September or October came. One day, the Librarian met Parthasarathy.

Parthasarathy.—Professor is leaving for India.

Librarian.—When?

Parthasarathy.—Next week.

Librarian.—Who will help me thereafter? (Laughter)

Parthasarathy.—It does not matter. I shall be staying back.

23 A Measure of the New Sense of the Value of Documentation

By that time, they had begun to make titanium diamonds — small pieces of diamonds. They were sent for sale in different markets. Those diamonds competed very well with the carbon diamonds. After some time, they withdrew those small pieces of diamonds. They wanted to make big diamonds. It appears that the Chief had been growing as big a Diamond as possible to be presented to the author of the C C.

Librarian.—Our Chief wants to present you with a Titanium Diamond. He has been growing it for this. He wants to make it very big. But, you are now leaving USA. What am I to do, Sir?

SRR.—How long do you want me to stay here?

Librarian.—Until he grows the Diamond as big as he wants.

SRR.—Should I not go home? Am I to wait till your Diamond grows big enough?

She went and reported this to her Chief. She then came back with a Diamond to be presented to me.

SRR.—Thank you very much.

Librarian.—If you would stay here for one month more, it would have become a little bigger.

SRR.—The Diamond is so big even as it is. I have never come across such a big Diamond. Thank you very much. But, I never accept gifts; and so, I shall give this over to my Government to be kept in our National Meseum.

Librarian.—No, no, Sir. My Chief will send another Diamond to your Government.

SRR.—There is a great physicist in our country, who is a specialist in diamonds — Sir C V Raman. I shall give this to him.

Librarian.—My Chief will send another Diamond to him! (Laughter).

Finally, she forced the Diamond on me. I brought it home. It was lying in our house till last year. We did not know what to do with it. One of my friends, Seshachalam, made a big ring for the use of my wife. My wife said, "How can I wear such a big Diamond ring and walk about with it?" So, she did not use it. "What to do," was the next question. Then, like a pious Hindu lady, she said, "No, no, we cannot have it in our house. Let us present it to the Parthasarathy Temple, Triplicane, in Madras, so that it can be made into a jewel for the Goddess Rukmini." Well, this was done.

3 Savings in Research Potential Through Documentation

I have just told you this experience to show how much a real business man has begun to value documentation. He has begun to value it because it saves him money. Look into Table 8 given below:

Table 8: Savings in Research Potential through Documentation

SN	Saving	Field of research	Country
1	Rs 1,650,000	Electronic welding equipment	Lithuania
2	Rs 8,000, per annum	Handicrafts	Sweden
3	Rs 100,000	Clothing	Denmark
4	Rs 300,000	Machine tool	India
5	500 man hours of research personnel	Research and development laboratory	USA

4 Invoking God's Aid

41 The Time to Think of God

When loss occurs man feels, "What are we going to do?" The scientists feel "What are we going to do?" As usual, when we are in difficulties, in whatever country we live, whatever be our tradition, when we are at the end of our tether, we think of God! (Laughter). I am glad that we think of Him at least on that occasion (continued Laughter).

42 An Analogy from Mahabharata

I shall now remind you of an anecdote from the *Mahabharata.* It is about Kunti. Do you know who she was (Voices. — "The mother of the Pandavas"). Do you know the name of the *Avatar* of the Lord, who played an important role in the Mahabharata War?" ("Voice.—Krishna"). Before departing, the Lord assembled everybody together.

The Lord.—Each one of you ask for a boon.

Some.—We want wealth.

Some others.—We want children.

Many.—We want continuing prosperity.

Kunti.—I want difficulties (all the others laughed on hearing this).

The Lord.—Kunti, explain to these laughing people why you asked for difficulties.

Kunti.—Krishna, it is only difficulties that will make me think of You.

The Lord.—You have heard Kunti. I am sure that you have also learnt something from her words.

43 Churning the Milky Ocean: Kurma-Avatara

Here is a Puranic analogy. According to *Bhagavata Purana* on an earlier occasion, a group of persons in difficulties joined together, and prayed to God, by singing hymns from Purusha-Sukta.

The Group.—Oh, Lord! Why are you lying on your leafy float drifting along in the midst of the ocean? We are all suffering.

The Lord.—Why do you bother? I am here by you. What do you want.

The Group.—We have difficulties in churning the Milky Ocean.

Then the Lord helped then in churning the Milky Ocean. I hope you know the story. The Lord came as a Kurma — a tortoise. The churn was a parvata — a mountain — that had got stuck up in the mire. As a tortoise the Lord went underneath the water, lifted up the mountain, and bore it on his back. To prevent it from wobbling he put one of his hands on its top, and made it steady.

5 Churning the Ocean of Subjects

A group of business men, scientists, and library scientists collected together, and prayed to God in the traditional way.

The Group.—You helped our ancestors out of their difficulties in churning the Milky Ocean. This time we are not churning the Milky Ocean. We are now churning the Ocean of Subjects. And we do not know how to do it. What are we to do? We are trying to classify, catalogue, and so on. It does not give us proper results. We do not know what to do. Please come and help.

The Lord.—Why are you bawling so loud? I am always by your side. Don't you know? You forget that I am always inside you. But, you bawl out as if I were far far away. All right, this time I need not come to you as a Kurma. I shall give this Tool. Take it with you and use it. With it you can make your churn work steadily.

Research was the churn; and Documentation was the Tool.

CHAPTER n

QUARREL ABOUT THE AGENCY FOR DOCUMENTATION

1 Apple of Discord

According to the Bible, when the first apple was produced, it caused discord between Adam and Eve — husband and wife. At that time, they were the only two persons in the world. Even then quarrel began. But there were two groups of persons — Scientists and Library Scientists — when the Tool of Documentation was got — and not only two persons as at the time of the first apple. The inevitable quarrel between the two groups of persons should have begun on a large scale.

2 Delay in the Starting of the Quarrel

Fortunately the quarrel did not arise for some time, because the group of scientists alone handled the tool. For, till about two decades ago, a library scientist was satisfied merely with doing public library work — such as handing over whole books and whole periodicals and helping a reader in selecting this fiction or that fiction. They neglected the research workers and did not do anything of Documentation at all. Therefore the scientists thought, "We know how to help ourselves." The tradition in the university libraries, used by them, confirmed this attitude. For, the professors were dominating over the librarians and did not allow them to develop or to do anything other than the traditional library work.

3 An Illustrative Anecdote

In March 1925, I was visiting the libraries in Edinburgh. At that time, Sir E T Whittaker, my Professor's Professor in Cambridge, was Professor of Mathematics in the Edinburgh University. As I had read his books as a student, which were all brilliant, I called on him one morning.

Whittaker.—Edward used to write to me that you were good in mathematics. And that you were the most promising of his students. Why have you run away from it?

SRR.—I was first unwilling to accept my appointment to the post of University Librarian, just then created. However, my Principal, a Scotchman, advised me to join the post, to have the advantage of travelling to other countries and if I still did not like it, he would take me back into the College. For the last six months, I have been studying the Library System of UK.

Whittaker.—What is there to study in this?

SRR.—I may mention at least one library discipline which is as good a challenge to the intellect as Mathematics.

Whittaker.—What! What is the wonderful discipline?

SRR.—Library Classification.

Whittaker.—What! Classification! How can you classify a book? How, for example, will you classify "Whittaker's *Modern analysis*?"

SRR.—Sir, it is a multi-focal book. I would put the whole book in the class "Functions of a complex variable." I would give a cross reference entry for each of the functions so beautifully developed in that book. Here are the class numbers, Sir:—

B38	Complex variable
B39	Special function
B391	Elementary function defined by a finite number of algebraic operations
B392	Integral of algebraic function
	Subdivision by chronological device (Illustrative)
B392L	Hyperbolic function
B392L8	Elliptic function
B392M	Hyperelliptic function
...	... ...
B2991	Function qualitatively defined
B399M	Meromorphic function
B399N	Quasi-analytic function
B399N2	Almost periodic function

Whittaker.—Is all this possible? I did not know about this. I wonder why our University librarian has not classified our books?

SRR.—I had been to your University Library yesterday. I was surprised to find all the books arranged alphabetically by the names of authors.

Then the following conversation between the librarian and myself took place.

Nicholson (Librarian).—I have heard from some of my friends in London about your attempts to design a new scheme for Classification based on Meccano-Principle.

SRR.—Why have you arranged your books alphabetically?

Nicholson.—The Chairman of the Library Committee is a strong-willed Professor. He said that Classification was nonsense and that it was impossible. Arrange the books alphabetically!

After hearing about this dialogue between Nicholson and myself, Whittaker resumed his conversation with me.

Whittaker.—You are now speaking to that very strong-willed Professor. Go and tell Mr Nicholson, the Librarian, that his strong-willed Chairman has now been converted.

But Prof Whittaker had not for long forgotten his defeat. In 1937, driven by communal passion and under misguided advice, the University of Madras ordered me to print the Catalogue of the Library, in order to make it possible to catch me, in case books were lost. I may say, as an aside, that it was a member of the Library profession that had given this advice to the University (Shame). But even the darkest cloud has its silver lining. So it was in this case. In 1938, I sent to Prof Whittaker a copy of the printed classified catalogue of the accessions of the year 1939. His eagle eye found in it an entry on "Wave mechanics." Then he examined the Mathematics part of the catalogue. Then began the following correspondence.

Whittaker.—I find that you have provided for the new subject "Wave mechanics" in Physics. No doubt, it is a subject in Physics. But what about the still more new subject "Wave function"? I do not find a number for it in your Catalogue.

SRR.—When the 1939 catalogue was printed I had not come across any book on "Wave Function." But a book on the subject has just now arrived. It is put under "B8 Physico-mathematics." Its class number has been fixed as "B85." In this class number the digit "5" is a mnemonic digit to represent "Wave." My Scheme has many such mnemonic uses of digits.

Whittaker.—Have you? My long lingering doubt about the possibility of classification, and the discipline of library classification being as good a challenge to the intellect as mathematics itself, is now finally gone. I stand totally converted.

4 Library Profession Woke-Up Too Late

The professor did not help the industries. Then the workers in industrial research said, "What are we to do? Well, we shall set apart some of our own research workers to do this job of documentation." They started doing this Of course, they knew how to do research in their respective subjects; but did not know how to do documentation. They thought that with their common sense and with their intimate knowledge of the subject, they could do some kind of documentation. They went on doing it. Eventually this made them to say "It is our right to do it. No one else can do it." It happened that the library profession woke up after they began to say so. They felt, "Oh! We have been neglecting a very good opportunity for us. We ought to get in. It is our job. Our work is, not merely to dole out books. We must be of help also in the development of micro subjects forming the field of research." The library profession entered the field of Documentation rather too late. Therefore, they had to face a fight with the scientists already engaged in Documentation. To some extent I was a witness to that fight; and in a sense I had also a personal feel of it.

5 Library Profession Elbowed Out

51 Atlanta City Episode

In 1950, the Special Libraries Association of USA was holding its Annual Conference at Atlanta City. Somehow they invited me. Probably they thought that I was a scientist and not a librarian. When Parthasarathy and myself were entering the Conference building, there was a small group of people standing outside. They were all librarians. One of them called Parthasarathy, because he looked younger than me.

Librarian.—We are all very proud of your Professor.

Parthasarathy.—What is the matter?

Librarian.—We had been elbowed out by the scientists from the new field of documentation. This is the first time we have dared to come to this Special Libraries Association.

Parthasarathy.—Why?

Librarian.—Your Professor is the first librarian to be invited by this Association. We have therefore made bold to come.

Anyow I spoke. I was accepted. It was all done. But that is not the whole joke. I had gone there that year to study the industries for seven or eight months. I wanted to know what kind of service the industries require from libraries. It was for that purpose that I went. I visited several industries.

52 Texas Oil Company Episode

I went to the Columbia University and asked my friend, a professor in its Department of Library Science:

SRR.—Look here, I have observed documentation work in many industries. But I have not yet seen an oil industry. Can you put me on to any Oil Industry Office where documentation work is done?

Professor.—Oh yes. It is easily done. There is the Texas Oil Company in this very city. I shall introduce you to its documentalist.

He then picked up the telephone and called the documentalist.

Professor.—Professor Ranganathan, from India, wants to see your library and documentation unit. Would you care to have him?

Documentalist.—Certainly.

SRR.—Why did you mention me as Professor Ranganathan? I am a librarian. I am proud to be called a librarian instead of a professor.

Professor.—No, no. When you go over there, you will know the reason.

I did not know for what it was. Anyway I went there and the documentalist received me with great respect. He showed me a long battery of cabinets containing documentation entries in cards, with subject indexes, subject headings, and so on. I went on seeing them. I found certain things beautifully done. It was really beautiful.

SRR.—You have done it wonderfully, Sir.

Documentalist.—Sir, who can do this, except an oil technologist? In Columbia University, those boys and girls go and study for one year, and then come out and say that they are librarians and they can do documentation work. What can they do, those little fellows?

Well, I was very patient (Laughter). I did not lose my temper. I was hearing him, whatever be the abuses, flowing from him as the names of the Lord in the *Sahasra nama* (hymn of a thousand names to denote God) (Laughter).

After I passed through 10 or 12 cabinets, I found a particular heading. But its synonym had also been put in the very first cabinet.

SRR.—Sir, I find that you have put the same subject here as well as there. How will your readers get them?

The documentalist examined and examined.

Documentalist.—I have really made a mistake. But how did you find it out, Sir? (Laughter).

He did not wait for my reply.

Documentalist.—You must be a very acute professor of technology, to know all these things. You know all these things?

I was not sure whether the time had come to tell him the truth about myself.

SRR.—I found it by Facet Analysis.

Documentalist.—Facet Analysis? You learnt Facet Analysis? Do you teach Facet Analysis? But, my Professor of Oil Technology never taught me facet analysis (Laughter).

SRR.—My dear friend, this facet analysis is in library science.

Documentalist.—But how did you know it, being an oil technologist?

SRR.—I am the author of it.

Documentalist.—What! A professor of oil technology author of Facet Analysis?

SRR.—I am really a professor of Library Science, and a Librarian. I am not a professor of oil technology, as you had been assuming.

You can understand his discomfort. He repented for all the abuses he had showered on my profession. But he was a very good man. He had a first class list of isolates for oil technology as subject headings for which I had been on the look-out.

SRR.—Sir, can you give me a copy of your list?

Documentalist.—It is a confidential document (Laughter). However, I must give it to you, because you showed me that mistake. Please keep it confidential.

6 Old Image of a Librarian: Civil War in the Library Profession

Little by little the librarians began to gain ground in the fight with scientists. But, civil war began among the librarians themselves. The documentalists regard themselves as belonging to a new profession. They look down upon the librarians and equate them with their old old image of a librarian in a public library, just putting date stamp and doling out books across the counter, or buying and accessioning books, and giving a strict account of all the books acquired.

7 The Claim of Documentalist

The documentalists claim that they are doing a piece of work totally different from that of librarians. They do not at all want to call themselves as librarians. They do not want to include their subject in the term 'Library Science'. They even invent new names for their 'New Subject' such as 'Information Science' and 'Informatics'. They call themselves 'Information Scientists' in preference to 'Library Scientists'. This creates a self-deception in them. They imagine that changing the label on a bottle necessarily means change in its contents.

8 Implications of the Five Laws of Library Science

The self-deception of the Information Scientists is due

to their not having understood the implications of the Five Laws of Library Science, in the setting of the present day society. Their mistake lies in their inability to interpret the term 'Book' in the Five Laws, in the light of the context of today. They are still imagining that a "Book" means a fairly stout volume that can fill the hand. They forget that even in the past, the term 'Book' had meant also a few sheets of paper stitched together, and given to the child as a Book. A few sheets of paper stitched together was also taken as a Book, for the use of the specialists. Do you know what such a 'Book' was called?

Voices.—Reprint.

SRR.—Reprint from what?

A Voice.—From a periodical.

SRR.—Why was it not printed directly as a child's book? What was the need first for printing it as a paper in a periodical and then to take a reprint of it?

(No reply from the audience).

SRR.—It was due to economic reasons. A child's book will sell in thousands of copies; but a thin book containing just one paper cannot command an economic market. Therefore, all such thin books for specialists have to be first produced collectively in a host periodical, from which a few copies of reprints can be taken in the measure of demand. If this meaning of the term 'Book' is understood according to Law 2 of Library Science, every reader should be served with his "Reprint" or in the absence of reprint with the "Paper in the periodical." It is the latter that happens more frequently. This should be done witout any loss of time in order to satisfy Law 4. Again, this should be done in spite of the papers in periodicals even on a single subject, running to thousands. Therefore, Documentation Work and Documentation Service, are complelling implications of the Laws of Library Science. And Documentation is an essential function of the Library Scientist. Of course, this new function has been realised only in recent years. Therefore, to emphasise this new function and to fix it in the minds of librarians the term 'Documentalist' is used to describe the librarian at the moment when he is doing Documentation Work or Documentation Service as it is in its Stage 4 (*See* Sec h4). In Sec g12 it has been stated that in order to eliminate multiplicity of terms, we shall use the term 'Documentation Service' to include also the term 'Reference Service'. For, the two denote the same purpose and their difference consists only in the degree of intensity of service. For a similar reason, we use the term 'Documentalist' instead of the term 'Librarian', whenever expedient.

CHAPTER P

DOCUMENTATION SERVICE: SUMMUM BONUM OF ALL LIBRARY WORK

1 Library Education: Generally Truncated

In many of the library schools in the world, library education is in the truncated form of teaching a bundle of discrete routines, without any attempt to unify them, and to present them as implications of some fundamental laws or normative principles. At any rate, this is what I experienced when I took the course in 1924-25 in the School of Librarianship of the University College (London). Perhaps, even today, library education in many of the library schools in the world is not very far from that state.

2 Effect of Earlier Experience in Education

I have had intensive experience in the educational profession for seven years before changing over to the library profession. While in the former profession, I had experienced year after year the effectiveness of developing every subject and even each topic within a subject from some appropriate fundamental principles of a general nature. Probably, this made me feel the consequences of the absence of normative principles to be used as the starting point in teaching Library Science and Practice.

3 Effect of Experience as a Student of Science

In my college days I had been a student of Mathematics and Physics. This experience induced in me a sense of revolt against having to hold in memory and deal with myriads of unrelated pieces of information and independent types of practices, as the teaching method found in the London School made us to do.

4 Traditional Method of Examination

The traditional method of examination in UK and in

India generally consisted of testing the memory of a candidate in holding isolated principles and practices. I revolted against this also. Even in Papers in Mathematics, I used to include one or two "Essay questions," in which a candidate had to show some given results as implications of some fundamental principles mentioned in the Paper. But I had also to give the traditional type of questions. A candidate was allowed to confine himself only to the "Essay questions." When I was living in Zurich from 1954–56, I found that the examination system in the Federal Institute of Technology was even better, though it had to be spread out over a month. The professor would meet a group of half a dozen candidates in about six sessions, spread over three consecutive days. The professor will start discussion on some topic on the subject of the examination fixed for the day. If necessary a candidate was allowed to look up a reference book or a formula. He was even allowed to derive his results from some basic principles, writing out on the black board the successive steps in his inference. Even if he did not remember a formula, but could deduce it only from the fundamental laws, he was in no way penalised. I was delighted to see this system. "True education should aim at this" I said to myself.

5 Curiosity to Find some Fundamental or Normative Principles

The experience mentioned in the preceding section came to me only in 1955. However, while studying in the London School of Librarianship in 1924-25 questions such as the following began to simmer in my mind:

1 Cannot all these empirical aggregates of information and practices be reduced to a handful of basic principles?

2 Cannot the process of induction be applied in this case?

3 Cannot all the known practices be got by the process of deduction out of the basic principles?

4 Do not the basic principles contain, as necessary implications, many other practices not current or known at present? and

5 Will not new practices become necessary, as and when the boundary conditions, set by society, change?

In the present context, we have seen how increase in population pressure has made documentation to be included as a necessary part of library work.

6 Sprouting of the Normative Principles in 1928

From the middle of 1925 to the middle of 1928, my thought had to be totally turned on the organisation of the Madras University Library from scratch. This drove the curiosity to the sub-conscious level and there it lay as it were in incubation. About late in 1928, after a few days of intensive travail, the Five Laws of Library Science sprouted. These Laws were first expounded before an audience of about a 1,000 teachers, assembled in the Annual Conference (Dec 1928) of the South India Teachers Union, of which I had become a member while in the teaching profession. These Laws were well received by the teachers. When I started the Madras School of Library Science in 1929, the education in library science was based on these Five Laws, and this gave satisfaction to myself and to the students.

7 Pictorial Representation

The picture of a Tower given on p. 71 is a symbolic representation of how all the diverse library practices — including documentation service (denoted by its old equivalent Reference Service) — are built upon the Five Laws of Library Science as the foundation. At the bottom of the

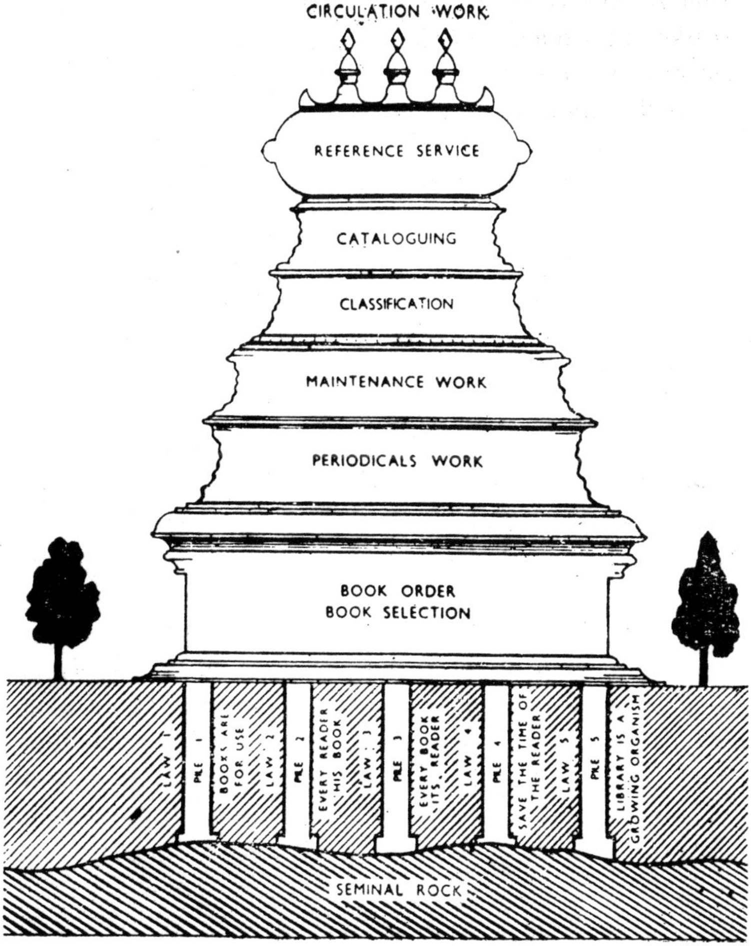

picture these Fundamental Laws are represented as if they were the pile foundations of library science and of all library practices, touching the primordial rock, as it were. Documentation Service (denoted by its old equivalent 'Reference Service') is shown near the very top. It is coupled with the routine of Circulation Work in which the document selected by a reader in the course of documentation service is allowed to be taken out for study by the reader. In sequence of time, this trivial routine has necessarily to come after Documentation Service. But, it can be realised without any difficulty that Documentation Service is the *Summum bonum* of all other items of library work. These items of library work are represented as layer over layer in the picture of the tower, in proper sequence, between the Five Laws of Library Science at the bottom and Documentation Service at the top.

8 Result of Not Knowing the Five Laws of Library Science

The falling over on Documentation by the scientists themselves was, no doubt, due to the library profession not recognizing its advent as a result of social pressure. But, when the library profession woke up later, and claimed to take charge of Documentation as its own duty, the scientists resisted this claim. One reason for this resistance might have been due to the adage "Possession is nine points in Law." But this would have been too trivial for the scientists to use as the reason for their resistance. My conjecture is otherwise. The true reason should be traced to a scientist not having been familiar with the Five Laws of Library Science and with the *Summum bonum* of all library work being Documentation Service as a compelling implication of the Five Laws of Library Science.

CHAPTER q

DOCUMENTATION SERVICE: HUB OF ALL LIBRARY WORK

1 A Pictorial Representation, in the form of a Wheel, of the Diverse Items of Library Work

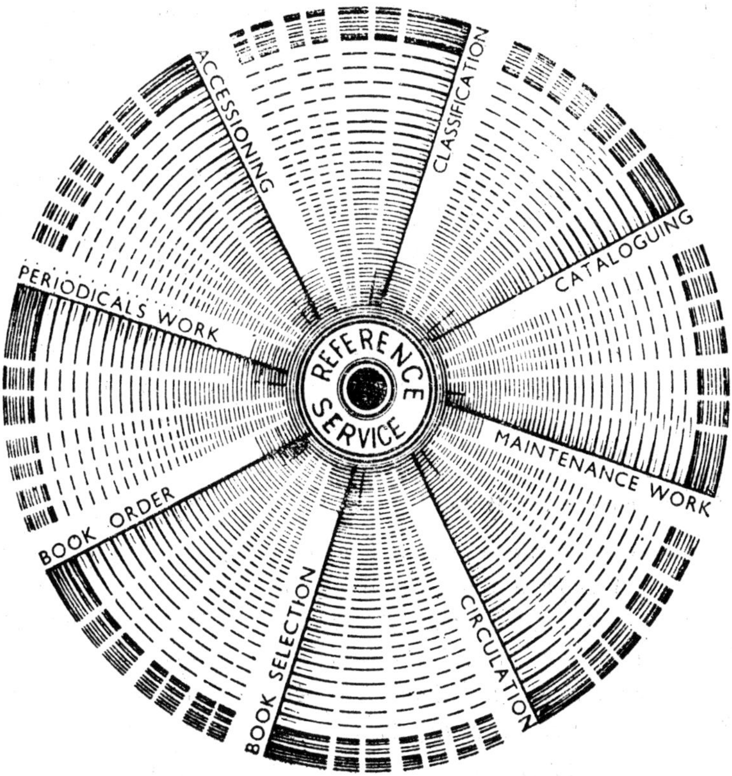

2 Absence of a Full Sense of Holism in the Students

As stated in Sec p1, in the School of Librarianship of the University College (London), I was exposed to the teaching of the diverse items of library routines as if they were a bundle. My mind reacted badly to the items of library routines not having been presented as compelling implications of some fundamental laws. When I started my School of Library Science in 1929, no doubt, I based the development of Library Science and of the diverse items of library routine on the Five Laws of Library Science. However, I had still some dissatisfaction. I realised that in spite of the items of library routine shown as implications of the Five Laws, the students did not have a full sense of holism in respect of the items of library routine.

3 A Hub to Tie up all Items of Library Work

I felt that the sense of holism would come if and only if all the items of library routine could be linked up into a unity. My imagination led me to think of a wheel with all its spokes organically linked to its Hub and thereby linked to one another. What can be the Hub? Should we look for it outside the diverse items of library work? Or does any one of the library practices qualify to be regarded as the Hub of the wheel instead of being taken to be one among the other spokes?

4 Search for the Hub

To answer the question mentioned last in the previous section, I searched for the Hub from among the diverse items of library practice. After a detailed examination it was found that none of the following library practices could hold together all the others, get all of them attached to it, and thus function as the Hub:

1 Book selection;
2 Book order;
3 Periodical publications work;
4 Accessioning;
5 Classification;
6 Cataloguing;
7 Circulation work;
8 Maintenance; and
9 Other usual office routines to be done in a library.

5 Seed of Divine Curiosity

While I was in the profession of education, I had learnt from practical experience that,

1 Education should, in the last resort, be self-education;

2 Curiosity is the stimulus to self-education;

3 The essential function of the teacher should be to rouse the curiosity of the students; but

4 The stimulus for curiosity differs from student to student;

5 It is possible to rouse the necessary curiosity for self-education even in the so-called "Un-educable" or "Dull" students.

It is this experience that made me appreciate the significance of the term 'Divine Curiosity' used by the great physicist Albert Einstein. I felt that the Hub should be one that can satisfy the Divine Curiosity.

6 What about Documentation Service being the Hub?

61 Theory of Documentation Service Eliminated

From 1924 I have been paying special attention to reference service. Its theory was developed quite elaborately along with the students. It led us to understand the different psychological types among readers and the differences among documents as they figured in documentation service. But the theory of these factors did not appear to have any claim to be considered as the Hub.

62 Ready Reference Service Eliminated

Ready Reference Service is a meagre and primitive form of Documentation Service. This has been shown in Sec h3. Therefore it was eliminated without much difficulty.

63 POTENTIALITY OF PRACTICAL DOCUMENTATION SERVICE TO BE THE HUB

The persistence of educational psycholgy of curiosity led me to examine the potentiality of Practical Service — in the sense of Long Range Reference Service involving the search for the relevant, nascent micro documents to do service to a specialist reader — to function as the Hub. But I failed to examine this in 1929. But, by early 1930, I got into the full swing of practical documentation service; and I began to give clinical training to students in documentation service in the triangular setting of the documents in the stack room, the catalogue entries in the catalogue room, and the reader. This line of pursuit gave good hope.

7 Documentation Service is the Hub

Practical Documentation Service easily disclosed

71 The Richness and the Poverty of the library collection. This led the documentalist to help in document selection and to ask for the hastening of document order, order for abstracting periodical and of accessioning;

72 The Helpfulness or the unhelpfulness of the classification done. This led the documentalist to work with the classifier and also to promote developmental research in classification and thus help in the improvement of the work of the classification section.

73 The Inadequacies of added entries in the catalogue — particularly the cross reference entries (denoted by the term 'subject analyticals' in a dictionary catalogue). This led the documentalist to work with the cataloguer and wherever necessary and possible to do developmental research to improve the rules;

74 The Helpfulness or otherwise of the sequence in which the Main Subjects are arranged. This led the documentalist to work with the Maintenance Section;

75 Groups of seldom-used documents obstructing a helpful continuous browsing of the documents in current use. This led the documentalist to work with the Maintenance Section.

Thus practical documentation service brought the students to see its being linked up with every other item of library work as the spokes of a wheel are linked up to the Hub. It also roused curiosity in students to understand the effects of the various library practices and to play a participative role in removing the defects in friendly co-operation with those engaged in the diverse library practices. Surely then Documentation Service is the Hub of all items of library practice if we take it in its entirety — its theory and its practice.

8 Focal Position of Documentation Service in Library Work as a Whole

81 Claim of the Scientist

The preceding section has shown in detail the focal position of documentation service among the diverse items of library work. The scientist should be made to know about this. If this be done he will not insist on documentation service being his exclusive province. There are signs that the scientists are now withdrawing from this essentially library work and going back to their own legitimate work.

82 Collapse of Claim of Documentalist of Another Species

After the scientists withdrew from the field, a new species of claimants has arisen for the exclusive possession of documentation service. These claimants even tend to put up an air of superiority and to look down upon the members of the library profession. They would reduce the work of the librarians to the status of mere clerical work to be done *behind* the screen. But they want it to be done, before they themselves can present the results as documentation service by working with the readers *before* the screen. This species of documentalists is not made up of scientists, but of those working in specialist libraries and designating themselves, not as librarians, but as "Information Officers." An amusing situation arose in the International Conference on Scientific Information, held at Washington from 16 to 21 November 1958. An Information Officer presented a draft syllabus for the training of documentalists, as if it were different from the syllabus for the training of librarians. After his presentation, I read out, one by one, each section of his draft syllabus and the corresponding section in the typical syllabus in vogue for the library profession. At the end I asked the Information Officer to point out where the difference lay between his draft syllabus for documentalists and the syllabus current for library profession. I also asked the conference not to confuse issues by drawing unnecessary and non-existing distinctions between librarians and information officers. The elasticity of humour of the "Information Officer" was so great, that he promptly stood up and said in effect, "There is no difference. I brought up this draft syllabus only to provoke discussion." (Laughter). Such was the collapse of the second species of documentalists — calling themselves "Information Officers."

83 Claim of "Information Officers"

Sec 7 of this Chap has given a true picture of the focal position of documentation service among the diverse items of library work. It shows that the work of documentation service is inseparable from the other items of work in a library. The "Information Officers" should know about this. If they do so, they will not insist upon calling themselves a new profession, different from the library profession. They would coin terms such as 'Information Officer' and 'Informatics' in their anxiety to keep themselves out from Library Scientists. Will they remember the collapse that happened in the Washington Conference? If they do, they will look upon themselves only as members of the library profession.

CHAPTER r

INDIAN TECHNIQUES OF DOCUMENTATION

1 Technique of Documentation

11 FACET ANALYSIS AND CHAIN PROCEDURE: THEIR INDIAN ORIGIN

Two essential techniques needed in documentation work are Facet Analysis for Classification and Chain Procedure for Subject Headings in the Catalogue. In documentation service also Facet Analysis is useful — nay, it is necessary. There is first the finding out of the reader's requirements in exact terms. For this the requirements of the reader, usually expressed by him only in inexact terms, should be facet analysed, with the cooperation of the reader. This has to be done in progressive stages of approximation. At each stage of getting a closer approximation, the class index entries derived by Chain Procedure and incorporated in the alphabetical part of the catalogue and the minutely classified sequence of the main entries and of the cross reference entries in the classified part of the catalogue are of immense help. Indeed, their use is essential. Both of these techniques were designed in India.

12 F I D AND FACET ANALYSIS

The value of Facet Analysis has been pointed out by the F I D Conference held in Brussels from 11 to 18 September 1955. The resolution passed on the subject was, "the F I D recommends that a deeper and more extensive study should be made of the general theory of classification, including facet analysis, and also of their application in the documentation of specific subject."

13 Dorking Conference and Facet Analysis

In its letter of 20 December 1956, the Organising Committee of the International Conference on Classification, held in Dorking (near London) from 13 to 17 May 1957, wrote to Insdoc, India's representative on F I D, "This Conference will be a development of all Dr Ranganathan's work in the last twenty years and will no doubt be a means of spreading interest in his work and appreciation of it." Further in its Concluding Session the Conference resolved that, "There is a general agreement that the most helpful form of classification scheme for information retrieval is one which groups terms [isolates] into well defined categories which can be used independently to form compounds and within which the terms [isolates] can be arranged in hierarchies."

14 Classification Research Group, London

"The enumerative schedules . . . fail to display correct relations between terms [subjects] . . . A type of schedule is needed which allows a genus to be subdivided in more than one way, to give several sets of sub-classes, each of which is a homogeneous group of collateral species. Such a schedule is in fact a faceted classification" (*Proceedings* of the International Study Conference, Dorking, 1957; P 137).

15 W C Berwick Sayers (U K)

In Sec 306.1 of his *Manual of classification*, Ed 3 1955, Sayers wrote, "The analytic and synthetic methods associated with C C have influenced recent classification study greatly even to fascination. [His] Octave Device, adopted by the International Federation for Documentation in 1948 for use with U D C is probably important."

16 D W Langridge (U K)

In page 317 of the *Library Association record* (71; 1969), Langridge states: "Ranganathan's classification theory and practice have influenced workers in Great Britain and in America. I believe that in the long term his own work will have greater importance . . . because of its coherence."

17 Harold Lancour (U S A)

In presenting Dr S R Ranganathan to the Chancellor of the University of Pittsburgh in 1964 for the conferring of the Honorary D Litt Degree, Lancour said, "His [Ranganathan's] explorations in the organisation of knowledge have led to the creation of a new approach to classification based on Facet and Phase Analysis. Indeed, upon his creative enquiry into the nature of documentation rests the structure of modern library classification."

18 E I Shamurin (USSR)

In page 326 of Volume 2 of his *Essay on the history of library and bibliographical classification* (1959) Shamurin writes, "Ranganathan aims to uncover the internal structure of the principles of the development of scientific library and bibliographic classification, providing . . . a correct deeply thought out organisation of recorded knowledge in all its divisions and subdivisions . . . Bypassing it and ignoring it, while developing new current scientific library classification, is impossible."

2 Curiosity of the West and Vatsyayana Analogy

Some Westerners used to ask me "You do not have much of industries or of industrial research in your country. The need for documentation has not yet arisen in your country. How is it that India has designed these two essential techniques of documentation?" I used to reply to them, "There is nothing unusual in this. Probably you do not know who wrote the first exhaustive treatise on Love and Love Making."

I wonder whether any of the members of this audience knows the name of the author of that classic produced centuries ago. (No answer). You take it from me. He was a bachelor. He was an Indian. His name was Vatsyayanā. When I tell them this fact, the Westerners feel amazed. Then they grant that there is nothing unusual in India having designed the essential techniques for documentation, even though it was virtually a "Bachelor" in respect of documentation.

3 Scoffing at Indian Techniques by Pre-Gandhian Librarians

Let us see how these techniques are being viewed by some old guards of the library profession in India without personal experience of documentation service to specialists — not even of ordinary reference service to generalist readers. "Oh, Faceted Classification. Absolutely useless. Who can look at it? What an ugly look a faceted class number has — comma, semicolon, colon, quotes, etc. Are these numbers?" These old guards grew mostly during the British period. They further say, "It is nonsense — Colon Classification. Look at the U D C number. It is all 1, 2, 3 etc."

My reply would be, "My dear friend, evidently you have not used even U D C in actual practice. If you have done so, you would not have missed the presence in the U D C numbers not only of letters of the alphabet but also non-numeral digits such as the punctuation marks, Colon, and Hyphen, and other digits such as Stroke, Inverted Commas, Circular Brackets, and even Square Brackets. So, according to your standard U D C is also nonsense.

Therefore you should only stick to D C in the belief that it can do anything. Try it by actually applying it to documentation work. You need not even believe the words of the editor of D C, that it is not intended for documentation work."

This allergy has been paraded in our country during the last ten years or so, by "Manager-Librarians" who have become seniors by efflux of time, and have begun to confuse the non-librarians in power and inhibit the younger librarians, by the exercise of their influence over the non-librarians who are the heads of the institutions of which the libraries form parts. Some are reported to have told some young librarians, "All these colon numbers should be wiped out within 24 hours." By ordering the beheading of C C, they imagine that I am myself being beheaded! (Laughter). They forget that it means nothing for me — whether you use C C or U D C or no scheme at all. I do not know why our country has developed such an antagonism to documentation techniques designed in India. Surely it could not have stemmed from a strict intellectual outlook. Is it caused by some lower emotions originating from the little ego?

4 Appeal to the Young Librarians of India

Here is an appeal to you. "Do not think that I am preaching for C C or any such thing. Unfortunately I am its author. If he (pointing to Prof Neelameghan) had talked about it, it would have been much better. Because I am the author, you may think I am an interested fellow. Probably you may think that I get some extra royalty for it (Laughter). Nothing like that, I may assure you. Whatever royalty I get, I give it away for some library purpose. One such is the Sarada Ranganathan Endowment for Library Science. Another had been the Endowment for the

Sarada Ranganathan Professorship in Library Science in the University of Madras. So I may assure you that I have no financial interest in "selling" CC. My interest is only a professional one.

5 Inherited Prejudice Against Indian Techniques

In our country, for about three hundred or four hundred years we have been lying in a sleeping phase — cultural sleep. We had to get everything from abroad. When I was young, my toys were all got from Japan, you know, as if we could not make them. Umbrellas were bought from Austria. Salt was bought from Italy. Yes, from all countries, except India! For a few centuries we have been habituated to this practice. That habit made us dislike anything that is Indian. That habit has been well embedded in our deeper sub-conscious levels. From there it continues to do mischief even today. Though it was inevitable, and perhaps even natural, during the British period, is it so today in Independent Renascent India?

6 Wrong Equation of Gandhi's Teaching with Khaddar

Gandhi appeared on the Indian scene about half a century ago. He did not call us fools. He said, "My dear children, this is a wrong attitude. You are now waking up. Why don't you make yourself self-reliant?"

What is the cult that Mahatma Gandhi introduced? "Swadeshi," is it not? "Prefer India-made commodities," he preached. But unfortunately, our people understood "Swadeshi" to mean only "Khaddar cloth" — cloth woven in India with the yarn hand-spun in India itself — and nothing else. Khaddar soon became a political symbol to seek independence. Then the full import of the term 'Swadeshi' was gradually forgotten. It even degenerated into a mere slogan.

7 A New Sense in New India

The time has moved still further. It has brought a new interpretation of Gandhi's preaching. This new interpretation was given by our Prime Minister, Indira Gandhi, in a speech she made about two years ago, in Bombay. She said in effect, "Now we have completed about twenty years of Independence. It is time that Gandhiji's 'Swadeshi' comes back to us in another way. It should apply not only to Khaddar and other material goods, but also to intellectual goods. We should respect ideas created in our own Motherland." A few days ago, I heard on the radio our Industries Minister at the Centre saying, "It is time that our industries develop our own know-hows; our own techniques; we have to stop the import of all these things unless we are not ourselves able to do them." Well, that is the new overall policy. This policy should also cover documentation techniques.

Do you agree or no? (Voices: "We all agree"). But what can the Government policy do in a democracy unless people cooperate and follow it? — If the old librarians continue to insist, "Any Indian Technique is of no use, it must be a foreign technique. Then only you will have your position safe in this country"? How many of you, librarians of renascent India, feel like those old librarians of Pre-Gandhian origin? (Voices: "None of us").

8 Melvil Dewey's Advice

Dewey himself advised me as follows, through correspondence, when he learned about my projected Colon Classification. In fact, I myself had written about my projected Colon Classification in my *Five laws* (1931) and I had sent him a copy of it.

Dewey.—You seem to be a young man. You are contemplating starting a new scheme for classification. It is very dangerous, I may tell you. I have paid heavily for having invented a scheme. It was our own profession that was responsible for this. But if you quietly adopt my own scheme, whatever happens, they will not blame you. You tell them it is the American Scheme. They will then say, "Beautiful"! (Laughter). Why do you start a scheme and lose your job? I know that my Scheme has not provided for Indian subjects. You give me the Indian subjects and their numbers according to the D C. I shall incorporate them in my next edition.

SRR.—It is not easy, Sir. I shall publish my Colon Classification, provide the Class Numbers, and then send it on to you.

Unfortunately he died before I could send it. Of course he meant it well and not with any kind of bad intention. He really did not want me to suffer in the way in which he himself had suffered, as a result of his having started the D C. If you do not know that, you read about it in his biography. Anyhow, I have been much more lucky. I have not suffered like Dewey. I have been living very happily in this country, in spite of having designed a new scheme and in spite of some Indian librarians decrying it. (Laughter). Anyhow, that is only an aside; because I see young faces here, who may be misled by the very noise of the cry against Indian techniques—Facet Analysis, Chain Procedure, Postulation Approach, and so on.

91 British National Bibliography Anecdote

One more story about it. Is Puranik here? Yes. Well, this morning he reminded me about it. Otherwise I would not have remembered. You know the *British national bibliography* which has been running since 1949. Its Editor, Jack Wells and I are friends. I used to go there every year and spend one or two weeks there and help them and so on. I am not saying this for pride. We are very good friends and were helping each other. He calls me "Ranga" and not "Ranganathan," and I call him "Jack" reciprocally. About ten or twelve years ago, I went to London. The following conversation took place between Jack and myself.

Jack.—Do you know a curious thing?

SRR.—What is it?

Jack.—A lady came from your country, deputed by your National Library, to learn the methods of building a national bibliography, classifying the subjects, and making subject headings, and so on. I asked that lady, "Have you come all the way from India for this? Have you not heard of the Chain Procedure? Have you not heard of Colon Classification?" She replied, "No, I have not heard of any of them. My Chief asked me to come and learn from you." I said, "Please go and tell your Chief that the methods adopted here are all Indian methods. (Laughter). The only thing is that we cannot use the Colon because Ranganathan has prohibited us from using it."

I did prohibit them because if they had adopted Colon, all of them would have lost their jobs immediately! Is it not so, Sir? Because in Great Britain, if they adopt a Scheme designed in their former dependency, all the fellows will lose their jobs. On the contrary, if you use an Indian scheme, you are threatened to be "fired." (Laughter). Because Puranik came and reminded me about it, I could tell you about this.

92 Faith in India's Capacity

I should now come to the last point. We have got a clean slate to write on, beginning in our own way. Remember Gandhiji's advice; remember Indira Gandhi's advice; remember the Industries Minister's advice. Keep all your windows open to get light from every country and from every part of the world. But do not think hereafter that there is only darkness within. Light can also be produced here.

93 Gentleman among Nations

India should be a "gentleman" among nations. If we take so much from England, we must give an equal amount to England. On the basis of such a reciprocity Independent India should grow hereafter.

CHAPTER s

HOW OF DOCUMENTATION: DOCUMENTALIST-READER RELATION

1 Reader is a Guest

I want to conclude with one last appeal to you. All these talks and all these conferences, will mean nothing to our country, unless each librarian devotes himself totally to his work. He should abstain from promoting or maintaining intrigues and quarrels, either within his library or within the profession at large. On the other hand, he should devote himself totally to the work falling to his share in building up the facilities for documentation service to readers — the *Summum bonum* of all the work in a library. The documentalist should receive his reader as his guest. In fact, you know our tradition. *Atithi Devo Bhava* — a guest is our God. I hope you all know this Upanishadic passage. The reader is your Atithi — Guest. He is God.

2 Conflict

SRR.—If a reader comes and the Chairman of your Library Committee also comes at the same time, whom are you going to serve first? That is my question. Let anybody answer.

A Voice.—Chairman.

SRR.—Reader first and not the Chairman. At that moment the reader is your guest and God, and not the Chairman.

A Voice .— We will ask the Chairman to sit on a chair.

SRR.—But to whom are you going to attend first, to meet his needs? That is the question. Those who will attend to the reader first, setting aside the Chairman, hands up please. Ajit, please count. Those who would attend to the Chairman first and then only the reader, hands up please. (Laughter). Tell me, if you are afraid of saying this way or that way (Laughter). I think you have got a sense of fear in you. So I take it that the neutrals, who form the majority, all want to say, "I shall first attend to the Chairman and then only to the reader." This is wrong. My appeal to you is not to do like that. First your reader, last your reader, and if any more time is left, attend to your Chairman, or the Committee Member, or to any such person.

A Voice.—If we do so, we lose our jobs.

SRR.—You are afraid that you will lose your jobs. If you are a coward, then do not become a librarian.

Another Voice.—Under the present service conditions in India, we have to serve the Chairman first.

SRR.—The present service conditions in India are made by you, young men. Why do you think that somebody is putting it over you? If you 200 people join together and all of you say, "I shall only attend to the reader first," who will remove all of you from your office? Tell me. You don't have that courage.

A still another Voice. — After hearing your speech, we will gather courage.

SRR.—Please think for some time and do not gather courage immediately and then let it go. (Laughter). Cultivate it in your mind; get convinced about it. Otherwise, I don't want you to do that. It will then end only as a disservice.

A Voice.—Theoretically, we are convinced.

SRR.—Theory by itself is of no use in the world, Sir. Will you be satisfied with theoretical food? (Laughter).

Another Voice. — Can we not treat the Chairman just like a reader?

SRR.—Yes, only if he comes as a reader. When the Chairman steps into the library not for that but says, "Do that, do this, my son is going for B Sc degree examination; he has not got the text books; buy a copy of each of the text books in your library for his use," do you call him a reader? On the contrary, if the Chairman comes as a reader, he is Atithi — he is guest and for the moment he is God. I am sorry. You have misunderstood my words, Sir, I don't say that because a man is the Chairman, he does not deserve at all to be attended to. He must be attended to if he comes as reader. But hardly any Chairman is a reader. (Laughter)

I think I have exceeded my time enormously. That is the cost you pay by asking an old garrulous fellow to come and speak. However, I cannot leave this topic without mentioning at least two ancedotes.

3 Glasgow Anecdote

I was in Glasgow in April 1925. The biggest city library there is the Mitchel Library. I called on its Librarian Mr Pitt. Just a minute earlier Mr Izett, the Chairman of the Library Committee, had entered the Librarian's room. Mr Pitt asked the Chairman to wait for some time so that he could attend to me. The Chairman agreed.

A Voice.—India is not Scotland.

SRR.—I little thought that you young librarians of the Gandhian period would still have this inferiority complex. Why should the standard of value in India be different from that in Scotland? Give up all such oldish notions of the British period.

A few minutes later Mr Pitt took me to the reading room. It was not an open access library. Therefore, every reader had to fill in slips for the books he wanted. At that time, a reader came to the counter. He had baggy trousers, and he looked like a workman.

Reader.—What a hell of time you take! How long am I to wait for my book?

Counter Assistant.—Your book has just arrived, Sir. It contains the slip given for it by you. The slip shows the time when you handed it over. Now please look at the clock. We have taken only five minutes to serve you.

Reader.—I am sorry. While waiting, time appears to fly fast. Is it not so? Please excuse me.

In that Library they have a time-piece. Its dial is made of hard rubber — the hour hand, the minute's hand, and the digits showing hours and minutes. When the next reader came and handed over his slip, the counter assistant banked the rubber dial on the inking pad and then on the application slip.

SRR.—Do you get such a time-piece in the market?

Pitt.—No. We get it made to order.

SRR.—Your assistant banks it on the inking pad and on the requisition slip with all the force given by the spring mechanism used by him. The time-piece cannot last long.

Pitt.—It is true. We have to get a new one every month.

SRR.—It would mean a considerable amount of money.

Pitt.—Yes, it is true. But that is money well spent. For, we have to respect our readers' needs — even their temper! You saw how that labourer flared up at the beginning, and how he quietened himself after seeing the impression of the time-piece on his requisition slip. Library exists for readers. We cannot afford to lose any reader. We must retain his custom, at any cost whatever.

Friends, you see, with what consideration even the poorest reader was treated by the Mitchel Library, as a Guest — as a God.

4 Delhi Anecdote

41 DELHI SEMINAR FOR LIBRARIANS OF SOUTH ASIA

In 1950, as a result of my persuasion, the Unesco helped in the establishment of a public library in Delhi, as a model for Asian Countries. In 1951 or 1952, I had gone out to Paris to attend a meeting of the Library Committee of Unesco. On the evening of the day I returned to Delhi, an Afghan and an Iranian librarian called on me.

42 STORY BY THE LIBRARIANS OF AFGHANISTHAN AND IRAN

The story narrated by the librarians of Afghanisthan and of Iran will shock you, I am sure.

Librarians.—During the last week we had been attending the Unesco Seminar on Libraries. The leader of the Seminar was the Librarian of the newly established Model Public Library in Delhi. Our main objective in coming to the Seminar was to meet you. We have known you only through some of your books — particularly the *Five laws of library science*.

SRR.—I am grateful to you for having thought of me.

Librarians.—When we came here, we were disappointed to know that you had gone to Paris. Fortunately, however, Mr Das Gupta, the University Librarian, told us that you were expected today. Therefore, we stayed back for two days.

SRR.—I am exceedingly glad to know that I have such friends in other countries.

Librarians.—In your *Five laws* we have read that the reader should be the first concern of a librarian — even in preference to the Chairman and the other members of the Library Committee. But, the leader of the Seminar said something very strange.

SRR.—What did he say?

Librarians.—He said "Don't believe in all that cult of Ranganathan. You must first exist before you do anything else. For that your first attention should be turned on the Chairman and the members of your Library Committee. Let the readers look after themselves"! We were very surprised when we heard it. We questioned him about this. But his naive reply was, "Ranganathan is a theoretician and not a practical man."

What do you think of this India's example? ('Shame!').

43 Repetition of the Appeal

May I repeat my appeal — Reader is your guest — your God. He should receive your first attention. Will you follow the example of Pitt or that of the Librarian of the Model Public Library in Delhi?

All Voices.—"Mr Pitt, beyond any doubt."

5 Librarian too Busy to Meet another Librarian

A year later, a librarian of Ahmedabad — an old student of mine — went to the Model Public Library, in Delhi, to study the working of its Children's Department. He had aready written to the Librarian about the day and time of his visit. When he went into the library, he was told by the orderly of the Librarian that his Saheb was very busy. Therefore, to save time, he went to the Children's Department and studied its working for about two hours with the help of the Children's Librarian, who was also an old student of mine. The Ahmedabad Librarian then went to take leave of the Delhi Librarian. Again the orderly repeated the same old story. Therefore, the Ahmedabad gentleman knocked at the door and went in. He found his colleague of the profession snoring deeply. He was leaning on the back of the chair with his legs propped up on his table. That is how he was busy! (Laughter). Smelling a stranger coming in, the Delhi Librarian became wild and shouted, "I do not want to be disturbed by you people. You are not my Chairman to come in this unceremonious way." ('Shame!').

6 Model Public Library Makes History

The Librarian of the Model Public Library in Delhi made history. His habit was to ignore readers and if any reader would not allow himself to be ignored, he would abuse him. It so happened that a Lecturer in a local institution was abused in this way when he asked the Librarian for some help. This lecturer sued him in a Court of Law for improper behaviour (Again, 'Shame!').

7 A Librarian Redeemed

I do not want to end with these pathological cases. Let me tell you how easy it was to redeem a reference librarian in the Public Library at Leeds. Its Chief Librarian had told me that he had posted a reference librarian in the stack room during rush hours, in the evening, to help the readers in the choice of their books. I visited that Library one evening. I walked into the stack room. I saw many readers helping themselves in finding their books. I thought within myself, "Is Law 2 of Library Science — 'Every reader his book' — to depend upon the reader himself for its fulfilment? What about the librarian put on floor-duty to fulfil Law 2?" I found one gentlemen looking out through a window. I guessed that he might be the reference librarian and I approached him.

Librarian.—I welcome you, Sir. Our Chief had told us about your visit. This evening I am the "Librarian-on-floor-duty."

SRR.—I am glad to know you. How is it that you are standing out here when there is such a crowd of readers?

Librarian.— I am too tired to work with them.

SRR.—When will you go back home?

Librarian.—At about 7-30, Sir.

SRR.—Will you still feel too tired to kiss your child and put him to bed?

Two years later, I happened to meet the Chief Librarian of that Library in London.

Chief Librarian.—Your question "Will you feel too tired to kiss your child" had a magic effect. From that next day my reference librarian did not "feel tired." He is all attention to readers.

SRR.—May God bless him. I had also told him, "The reader is your guest, your God for the time being. In the presence of God, all feeling of tiredness will evaporate away."

Chief Libraian.—He told me about it. These words converted him totally.

8 The Request

Ladies and Gentlemen, my final request to you is to treat every reader of yours as your guest and as your God for the time being. Though the anecdotes pertained to generalist readers in generalist libraries, their message is equally true in giving documentation service to specialist readers in specialist libraries. I shall next describe to you some traditional analogues to what should be the actualities in documentation service.

SRR.—How much time will you give, Ajit?

Ajit.— As much time as you like, but my concern is only your body being overstrained. I remember how weak you looked when I called on you two days back. But, here your weakness has been hidden by your enthusiasm. I do not want that there should be a breakdown in this meeting.

Chapter t

ANALOGUES FROM TRADITIONS

1 Analogy from Yajur-Veda

The *Taittiriya-Upanishad* of the Yajur-Veda contains the following passage, embodying exhortation at the convocation, on the eve of a batch of students entering life.

अतिथि देवो भव	The guest is your God
श्रद्धया देयम्	Serve him, with all attention
श्रिया देयम्	Serve him, to your utmost capacity
ह्रिया देयम्	Serve him with all modesty without any touch of ego or prestige
भिया देयम्	Serve him with a sense of fear, lest anything should go wrong
संविदा देयम्	Serve him with a full knowledge of his needs

We cannot find a clearer or fuller statement of the way in which documentation service should be given to a reader.

2 A Misfit for Documentation Service

In 1929, I had to recruit five fresh graduates and train them for documentation service in the Madras University Library. By 1930, most of them had developed satisfactorily. One of them, however, turned out to be a misfit beyond redemption. A young research student suddenly stopped away from coming to Library. I asked his Professor to send him on to me. He came to me.

SRR.—Why are you not coming to the Library nowadays?

Student.—Nothing, Sir.

SRR.—Your face shows that you are hiding something from me. Tell me the truth.

Student.—I am sorry, Sir. This would be saying something against one of your staff.

SRR.—It is your civic duty to tell me. Otherwise you deny to me the opportunity to improve the service of the library.

Student.—I asked for *ZDMG*. Your documentalist asked me what it was. I confessed that I did not know. He ridiculed me saying, "Without knowing this, how did you dare to take up research in Sanskrit? I wonder how your Professor tolerates you."

Ladies and Gentlemen, tell me what fault in the conduct of that documentalist brought the Library to the brink of losing an important reader — a valuable guest. I may tell you that that reader is now an eminent Professor in our country.

Voices.—Egotism of the lowest kind.

SRR.—Exactly. Egotism and prestige coupled with little knowledge. Remember Alexander Pope's line, beginning with "Little knowledge is dangerous." I had to take away that misfit from the work of documentation service. I assigned him to do book order work, and thus made him to work only "behind the screen," without any opportunity to come into contact with readers.

3 Analogy from Valmiki

Valmiki's *Ramayana* gives a delightful picture of the way in which readers should be given documentation service. The picture occurs in the description of the way in which Sage Bharadvaja served his guests in his entertainment to King Bharata and his retinue. The charming setting with flower trees and a green lawn, pleasant rooms, cosy seats, bright genial attendants here there and everywhere. There were sufficient number of attendants to provide each guest with an attendant all to himself — Api-Ekam-Ekam, one for each one. The attendant arranged for the bath, helped in dressing, and adorned the guest in his charge with flowers and so on. He also found out from the guest his exact taste and served him food to suit his exact taste. The picture mentions also cases of small groups being served together. All this points to the ideal to be reached by a library in serving its readers. I hope you will all emulate sage Bharadvaja when you go back to your library.

Voices.—We shall try our best.

4 Suggestion from Sanskrit Terminology

In Sanskrit,

41 'Laya' means "Integration"

411 'Ālaya' means "Perfect integration" — at-one-ment

412 'Ālaya' also means an "Abode" or a "Place"

42 'Grantha' means "an expression of an exposition of a subject — in other words, a "Work"

43 'Granthālaya' means a place where the mind of a reader gets integrated with an expression of an exposition of a subject; this is a "Library" in sense one

44 'Granthālayi' means a person at the head of or engaged in Library (in sense one)

45 'Granthālaya-kalā' means the library techniques necessary in a library (in sense one)

46 'Granthālaya-shāstra' means library science forming the basis of library techniques

47 'Anu-laya-sēva' means service in the integration of the mind of a reader with an expression of an exposition of a subject. This is one of the many library techniques — indeed the most important and ultimate technique, to facilitate which, all the other techniques are designed and followed — such as, Document Selection, Library Classification and Library Cataloguing. The term means "Documentation Service."

471 'Anu-laya-sēvi' means a person helping in the integration of the mind of a reader with an expression of an exposition of a subject. The prefix 'Anu' emphasises working with the reader with his cooperation — and not working on the reader. The whole term means "Documentalist."

48 'Pustaka' means a physical embodiment of an expression of an exposition of a subject — in other words "Book."

481 'Pustakālaya' means the place where books are housed — "Library" in the Chaucerian sense.

5 Analogy from Sri Aurobindo

The following is based on a digest of Sri Aurobindo's *Mother* (1928).

51 Cosmic Trinity

Cosmic trinity consists of

511 *Purusha,* the Divine Unmanifest;

512 *Prakriti,* Nature, particularly humans, standing in need of enrichment by *Purusha*; and

513 *Sakti,* the Energy Principle activating the descent of *Purusha* on to *Prakriti* and the ascent of *Prakriti* on to *Purusha.*

52 Sakti and Her Aspects

Sakti has four aspects:

521 *Mahesuxari*—Aspect of Wisdom. She opens us to the treasurehouse of knowledge. Partiality She has none. She deals with men according to their nature.

522 *Mahakali*—Aspect of Strength. To knowledge she gives a conquering might and imparts to the slow and difficult labour an impetus that multiplies the power and shortens the long way.

523 *Mahalakshmi*—Aspect of Harmony. Grace and charm and tenderness flow out from Her. Wherever She lets fall the loveliness of Her smile, the soul is seized and made captive and plunged into the depths of an unfathomable bliss.

524 *Mahasaraswathi*—Aspect of Power of Work. She is kind, smiling, close and helpful. Her eyes are on all needs at once. Her intuition knows what is to be chosen and what rejected, and successfully determines the right instrument. Her action is laborious and minute. The will in Her work is scrupulous, unsleeping and indefatigable.

53 The Analogy

The following are the analogies:

531 *Purusha* is *Akshara-Brahma*—that is, God in the form of an expression of an exposition of a subject.

532 *Prakriti* is *Manushya Prakriti*—that is, the human.

533 *Sakti* is the energy principle helping each expounded expressed subject to find its consumer or reader (Law 3 of Library Science), and helping each consumer or

reader to find his subject expounded and expressed to suit his needs (Law 2 of Library Science).

54 The Instrument of Sakti

The documentalist is the instrument of *Sakti* in bringing together each expressed expounded subject and its reader.

55 The Qualities of a Documentalist

The documentalist should develop the qualities represented by the four aspects of *Sakti* — Wisdom, Strength, Harmony, and Power of Work.

56 Source of Inspiration for Documentalist

The four aspects of *Sakti* should inspire a documentalist. This inspiration should embrace both his external doings and inner adjustment — that is, self-discipline and self-perfection.

57 A Documentalist and Force of Sakti

A documentalist should attune himself to the mission of *Sakti,* to Her Force and to Her *Ananda* (Delight). When this attunement becomes Entire, the knowledge, will, and action of the documentalist will become sure, simple, luminous, spontaneous, and flawless.

6 The Oldest Known Documentalist

China has a record of the oldest known librarian in the world. Its ancient philosopher Lao-tze is said to have worked as a librarian in his earlier years. Surely, in those days any library would have had only one librarian — a do-all librarian. We may believe without any hesitation that such a learned and wise librarian should have given the greatest weight to his function as a Documentalist. Blessed were the readers who used his library.

7 Documentation Service to Adi Sankara

There is a tradition recorded in one of the biographies of the great Indian Philosopher and Expounder of Monism — Sankara of the first millennium A D. He wished to write a commentary on *Lalitha-Sahasranāma* — the hymn of the thousand names of Goddess Lalitha. He asked his librarian to bring a copy of that work. When the librarian brought the manuscript, Sankara found it to be *Vishnu-Sahasranāma* — the hymn of the thousand names of Lord Vishnu. Sankara asked the librarian to bring the right book. Again he brought another manuscript of *Vishnu-Sahasranāma*. Sankara asked, "Did you not hear me properly?" The librarian replied: "There is a lady in the library. She gave these manuscripts, and asked me to tell you that you should write a commentary on this." Sankara's intuition flared up. He said, "The Goddess herself is doing documentation service to me. You are lucky, librarian, in having seen Her. Let us go to the stack room. I want to see Her and get her Blessings." But by the time they reached the stack room the Goddess had vanished away.

Moral: A documentalist should completely efface his ego. There should be no expectation of fruit; and no seeking of reward of any kind; and there should not be tarrying to receive a word of "Thanks." The only fruit should be the fulfilment of having served the reader in the precise measure of his needs at the moment, though he might not have expressed it correctly. The only reward should be a constant progression towards the attainment of the capacity to fulfil the Five Laws of Library Science, in "Perfect Perfection," as Sri Aurobindo would put it.

CHAPTER u

SALARY SCALE FOR LIBRARIANS

0 Questions From the Floor

My task is now over. Question time begins. You are welcome to put any reasonable questions relevant to the subject of my talk or to documentation.

1 Indian Library Service

A Voice.—Like I A S (Indian Administrative Service), can we not have an I L S (Indian Library Service)?

SRR.—I may tell you, Sir, that you have put this question evidently as a man who is suffering very much. It is a question of bread and butter. I shall begin by saying that service to the public and salary often have little to do with each other. The more the salary, the less the service given to the public! It may look strange. But this is what has often happened. I shall illustrate this.

2 Indian and Madras Educational Services

21 Experience with Principal 1

Some of you may remember that I began my career as a college teacher. On 9 July 1917, I entered Government service as assistant lecturer in Mathematics, in the Government College, Mangalore. It was a second grade college. There were only two classes in the Collegiate Department. I had therefore to do some Mathematics and Physics in the High School Department. My starting salary was Rs 70. The Principal was an Indian. He had only a B A degree, though I had an M A degree. But his salary was Rs 400 or more, because he had graduated from the Cambridge

University. He too was a Mathematics man. He wished to teach some Mathematics to the intermediate class. But he felt very diffident. It appears that, week after week, he used to collect some ideas from my predecessor and relay them to the class for about two hours in a week. He continued that practice in my days also. Further, week after week, he also used to collect some ideas from the assistant lecturer in English and relay them to the class for about two hours in the week. He thus went off with four hours of teaching in a week, whereas an assistant lecturer had to do 15 hours of teaching.

22 Experience with Principal 2

Two years later our College had another Principal. He too had a high salary; he too had taken a Cambridge pass degree. It was in Natural Sciences. He could not teach English. He could only teach Natural Science for four hours in the week. Here is a typical example of his method of teaching. One day he wanted to try teaching Physics to one of the high school classes. He asked me to be with him. I told him that the students were about to begin the study of "Light." He began with the question "How does light travel?" There was no answer. Then he asked, "Does light travel through the window, or through the door?" All the students replied "Through both of them." He then told them, "Say, light travels along a straight line." "How can we say that?" asked the students.

23 Explanation by the Principals

The Principals used to say that they did less teaching because they had administrative work. But, I could not find them doing administrative work even for one full hour on most of the days. Even for this little administrative work they used to take the help of one or another assistant lecturer, wishing to earn his good will. The Principals justified their higher salary on the ground that they had spent money in going to U K, whereas we had not!

3 My Visit to U K

After my appointment as University Librarian in January 1924, I spent a year in U K. While in U K, I was struck by the industry of the professors and of the members in the other professions. In those days they were normally working nearly 48 hours in a week. I used to find some of the professors of the University College (London), where I was taking my Course, coming to the College by 9 a m and leaving only after about 7 p m. This I found in most other places visited by me. I said to myself and also wrote to some of my friends in Madras that one of the main causes of U K being a rich world-power was the hard work put in by most of its people, and that one of the causes for our lying low was our evasion of work. After I came back home on 9 July 1925, I began to put in work for 8 to 10 hours a day in organising the University Library, in training the staff, in helping readers, in teaching library science for at least one hour a day, and in writing books and papers. This kept me busy the whole day-time.

4 Presidency Club Anecdote

About six months later, a visitor, belonging to the Educational Service, came to me.

Visitor.—I have come to you on behalf of the Presidency Club.

SRR.—What is that Club?

Visitor.—Have you not heard about it? It is a Club exclusively for "England-returned" men occupying positions as "Gazetted Officer" [as distinct from subordinate officers].

SRR.—Do you meet on Sundays and on other holidays?

Visitor.—No, no. We generally reach the Club at about 3 p m every day.

SRR.—How can you? Don't you have sufficient work in your offices?

Visitor.—You know that we are higher Officers. We do not have much work to do. It is mostly telling the subordinate staff what they should do, and signing the few letters going to higher authorities.

SRR.—What about the officers in colleges?

Visitor.—You should know about it. You had been a member of the subordinate staff in colleges, before you became the University Librarian. Don't you remember that you had to do most of the teaching and that the higher officers used to come to college at about 12 noon and to go away at about 3 p m after teaching for one hour some days, and two hours on certain other days?

SRR.—I know it. But I honestly feel that it was all wrong.

Visitor.—Let me tell you the mission entrusted to me by the other members of the Presidency Club. It is to invite you to join the Club.

SRR.—I am sorry. I cannot find time for it.

Visitor.—You have gone to U K. You are now getting a high salary as we are ourselves doing. You are the head of your Office. You should not work the whole day as you do.

SRR.—The work has to be done. How else can it be done?

Visitor.—You should leave it all to your subordinates, as we do.

Ultimately I was "excommunicated" by those august Officers for the following reasons:—

Reason one: I did not join the Club.

Reason two: I was not following the tradition of "England-returned officers." I had not maintained the status of an officer getting a high salary.

Reason three: I was also "fowling the nest" of the gazetted officers by setting a bad example!

5 The Poison Creeps into the Library

The poison had also crept into the less than half a dozen libraries in the country in those days, having librarians with a salary scale on a par with that of gazetted officers. Those librarians did hardly any professional work. They "administrated" the office. They too would come to the library by about noon and leave it at about 3 p m. They found ample time to move in "Society" and thus maintain a high "Status." Unfortunately, after the upgrading of the salary scales of librarians between 1947 and 1957, the poison has widely spread into many of the libraries of today.

6 A Question to the Gentleman Who Started the Question

Do you want an Indian Library Service to be formed to ensure a high salary and to keep up a higher status by finding ample leisure to become a Society man? Or do you want it only for freeing yourself from little worries due to pure salary, so that you can devote your full thought and time to the service of readers, and for that purpose to keep continually improving all the library techniques? If your interest is the one mentioned by me first, my vote goes against your proposal. On the other hand, if your interest is the one mentioned by me second, the first vote in favour of your proposal will be mine. I must now take the liberty of administering a warning against a danger with a great temptation-capacity. A new theory is now being adumbrated by some officer-librarians that the Chief Librarian should only be a good manager and a person who commands respect in society, but that he need not necessarily be good in library techniques, and that he need not even know library techniques; if he is an efficient manager he could drive his subordinates to do all kinds of technical work, including documentation service.

7 An Appeal: Prefer Professional to Managerial Work

An appeal to the younger persons in the profession. Do not swallow the dangerous theory abumbrated of late by some Chief Librarians. Even now they imitate their British Officers of their younger days in themselves doing as little work as possible, but driving the subordinate staff with smiles and threats. But you are men of the Gandhian period. You must take your professional work seriously. If your library is too large for you to do the professional as well as the managerial work, appoint a management expert to look after the administrative work under your supervision. But you must concentrate on professional work. That is what Mother India demands from you.

CHAPTER V

STATUS vs SALARY

1 A Wholesome Heritage

In my opinion, it is wrong to determine the status of a man by the salary he draws. Status is not something conferred on a person by others on the ground of his high level of salary. On the other hand, status is something earned by a person, whatever his salary is. He has to earn it by service to the public — service of the right kind. He has to earn it by his industry and his achievement. It is amazing how easily we forget the wholesome features of our heritage and even decry them as anachronisms not suited to modern times. Let me illustrate what little of positive correlation there need be between "Status" and "Salary scale."

2 An Advocate in Temper

The following anecdote belongs to the period before World War II. I was then Librarian of the Madras University Library. The man working next to me was getting less than eighty rupees per month. All the documentalists in the Library were then getting only a salary between rupees forty and eighty. Our Library was on the Marina Road in Madras — a long road facing the sea — a place of evening resort for the élite residents of the City of Madras — officials and non-officials. After their duty hours the documentalists of my Library used to walk home along the pavement on the Marina Road. They were not well-dressed. They walked bare-footed. They had put on only an half-armed shirt of thin cotton — their usual dress even in the Library. One day, a prominent Advocate of

Madras came into my room, with his temper almost at the end.

Advocate.—How much salary do you pay to your assistants?

SRR.—Why do you want that information?

Advocate.—Sir, we have been witnessing something, day after day, on the pavement of the Marina Road.

SRR.—What is it that has disturbed you so much?

Advocate.—Members of the Executive Council for the Governor stop for a minute, shake hands with your staff, and talk to them something for a minute or two. So do knighted gentlemen, and big businessmen. So also do judges of the High Court.

SRR.—Why should this disturb your mind?

Advocate.—All the while, we place ourselves at different vantage points in order to catch their eyes. But they never look at us. But they go on shaking hands with your ill-clad people. They totally neglect us with trim silk suit, stiff collar, silk tie, and laced turban! [Probably you do not know that in the British Period such a dress with stiff collar was the one considered as the dress of the gentleman of any worth. It is only after our Independence Pandit Nehru set a closed coat or a bush-shirt as the right dress].

SRR.—Their salary is between rupees forty and eighty.

3 Service Earns Status Better than Income

Advocate.—Is that all? But how is it "Big persons" shake hands with them, quite in the open?

SRR.—They do service to them — good book service and good documentation service.

Advocate.—I was under the impression that you have put all of them on a high salary.

SRR.—High social status and high salary scale do not always go together. They need not. You know the respect shown to Sri Ramanarshi. You know his status in society. What is his salary?

Advocate.—Do you suggest that high income is an obstacle to high status?

SRR.—No, not at all. On the other hand, I have been constantly endeavouring to put the library staff on a proper scale of salary. I have not yet succeeded. But I have every faith that as time goes on and as the great service being done by the library staff is realised widely, a higher scale of salary will fall on their lap, without any effort, even as a fully ripened fruit drops down from the tree.

Advocate.—I admire your optimism. I wish you success in your efforts.

4 Degenerate Scale of Value

I shall give you an experience of the opposite kind also, due to the prevalence of a low scale of value and a false measure for status. It was in 1928. Before that time there was hardly any library in Tamil Nadu with a competent staff giving service to readers. In May that year, I went out for some public contact work on behalf of the Madras Library Association. Dindigal, a taluk headquarters town, was in my itinerary. There were no hotels in such places in those years. There was no other go except to become somebody's guest. Therefore, Shri K V Krishnaswami Aiyer, President of the Association and a rich advocate of Madras, wrote to a relative of his in Dindigal, asking him to have me as his guest. He was the highest-paid officer in that town. He felt embarrassed when asked to take a librarian as a guest. I knew about it only after my train reached Dindigal at about 9 a m. As I was a stranger to my host, I thought that it would be wise for me to sit in my carriage till he would come and look for me. I heard a voice calling out my name and moving from the last carriage onwards. The platform was full of passengers. I expected to be released from the carriage by the host who was calling out my name. But to my dismay the voice stopped. After a few minutes it began near a few carriages ahead of my own. I asked a porter to run to the person calling my name and bring him to me. He came in a minute. His dress showed that he was perhaps a servant of my host. This he was. He took out all my luggage and put it into a single bullock cart and asked me to get in. The cart stopped in front of a big house. Then my escort told me: "Sir, please excuse me. Stay in the cart, I shall come back in a minute." He had evidently told his master that I was travelling in the First Class and that it might be improper to put me up in his own house.

Result: My luggage was taken into his master's house. I myself was asked to get down and go into the house. There I saw the "August Officer" sitting in his chair. He did not utter a word to me, but simply pointed to a room. I found my luggage in it.... Lunch time arrived.

Officer.—My servant told me that he found you in the First Class compartment.

SRR.—Yes.

Officer.—I did not expect a librarian to travel in the First Class.

SRR.—I am not surprised.

Officer.—You look too bright to be a librarian. What examination have you passed?

SRR.—M A examination.

Officer.—Then why did you become a librarian? Could you not get at least a teacher's post?

SRR.—Till four years ago I was Assistant Professor of Mathematics in the Presidency College.

Officer.—Why did you leave it and become a librarian? What a pity that this should have happened. Anyhow, what is your salary now?

When he found that my salary was much higher than that of his, he burst into saying "Look at the bad days to which we have come. We are wasting on a librarian's post not only an M A but also such an high salary!"

After this explosion he would even hesitate to sit when I was standing — status and salary!

5 Service of the Madras University Library Remembered Everywhere

The high quality of the service given by the documentalists of the Madras University Library is being remembered throughout India and abroad too. The Indian Civil Service persons of Madras, working in Delhi and other places, often speak to me in high terms about the fine library service they got in Madras. Even after 20 years, they still mention the name of each documentalist of Madras when they recall their services. When I visit an Indian Embassy in any country, I generally find one or two graduates of Madras in its staff. The first thing they ask me is, "How is Mr Sundaram doing?" — (He was the chief documentalist in the Madras University Library). "How is Mr. Ramabhadran?" — (He was the documentalist on duty in the morning hours). They add, "We can never forget the service we received from them." It was only two years ago that two members of the Indian Administrative Service (I A S) stationed in Bangalore, happened to meet me. Their enquiries and their feeling of gratefulness were exactly the same. They even added, "We owe to their service, our success in the I A S Examination!"

6 Effect of the Good Service done by the Madras University Library

A Voice.—How long is this low salary and high status to continue? A good salary alone can feed our children.

SRR.—I agree. I do not say that all librarians should for ever live like the *sanyasis* (holy men). On the other hand I am second to none in pressing on the authorities, "It is time that you make the Salary Scale of your Library Staff commensurate, not merely with the high social status gained by them but also to do justice to them, and also make them and their family live in comfort." I will soon tell you the story of how the excellent service given by the "ill-clad and poor-paid staff" of the Madras University Library forty years ago has been responsible for the high salary scale now obtaining for the librarians in our country.

CHAPTER w

LIBRARY STAFF OF GOVERNMENT OF INDIA

1 S O S from the Secretariat Library Association of Delhi

In August 1945 I had migrated to the Banaras Hindu University Library. The next year, I received an S O S from the librarians of the Government of India. On their behalf Shri Guha Roy wrote to me about their salary scale.

Guha Roy.—The first Pay Commission has been appointed by the Government of India. The Commission is not at all considering our position. We have no Godfather to present our case to the Commission. Please help us. We shall be ever grateful to you for this.

SRR.—How do I come in? I do not belong to the Library Staff of the Secretariat. I am an outsider.

Reply.—If you do not help us, who else can?

SRR.—There is only one way by which I can come in. You ask the Commission to put me some questions.

Reply.—How can we dare to approach the Commission with such a request? We do not have any status or influence to approach the Commission. But the Chairman of the Commission is Justice S Varadachariar. We learn that you two are good friends. You can certainly take the initiative and write to him. Further, the Chief Justice Sir Maurice Gwyer is a good friend of yours. We remember that you were his guest in 1942, when you came to Delhi for the first time. You came to advise him on the organisation of the Delhi University Library. We also remember his asking us to invite him to the Tea-party arranged by us to meet you at that time. You can ask him also to put a word to his colleague Justice Varadachariar.

SRR.—I am afraid that your personal interest in this matter makes you exaggerate the degree of my friendship with them!

2 Ultimate Success

Ultimately I yielded to their persuasion. The chief motive for this was that I regarded this request as the first God-sent opportunity for me to tackle the problem of salary scale, of at least one wing of the library profession of India. I started correspondence with the Chairman of the Pay Commission.

SRR.—Sir, you must do something for the librarians of the Government of India.

Chairman.—What do you want me to do for them?

SRR.—I wish that you bring up the salary of the Secretariat library staff on a par with a lecturer, reader, or a professor in a University, depending on experience and the kind of work to be done by the different members of the staff in the different libraries of the Secretariat.

Chairman.—Are you under the illusion that these people are giving the kind of service being given by your young men in the Madras University Library? Nothing like that here.

SRR.—The poor performance by the library staff of the Secretariat is due to the Government itself. It had fixed the salary scale for them at a very low level — much below Rs 200 per month. In a costly place like Delhi this salary can attract and retain only persons of that much intellectual calibre. How can we expect them to do any high class service? You say, "They do not give service, and I cannot recommend higher salary." I say, "Unless you give a high salary, you will not get proper men capable of doing proper documentation service."

This argument went on for some time. "Seed first or tree first," that was the question — a time-honoured conundrum. Ultimately, the Chairman agreed, and he did recommend my proposal to the Government.

3 A Safeguard

SRR.—The moment your recommendation is sanctioned by the Government there is going to be trouble. The clerical staff of the Secretariat are "close to the throne." They will mix up their own positions and those of the librarians and will divert to themselves all the benefits recommended by you for the library staff. Wherever vacancies occur in the Secretariat libraries they will manage to get into those places. The librarians cannot compete with them in fighting against such happenings, because they do not have as much access to the authorities as the clerks in the Secretariat have.

Chairman.—What can I do to prevent this? I quite see the danger. Can you suggest any way out?

SRR.—Yes. You recommend that the librarians should be put in a separate cadre of their own, and name it as "Academic Cadre" or "Technical Cadre" — quite different from the Clerical Cadre and from the Cadre of the hierarchy of Section-Superintendents, Under Secretaries, Deputy Secretaries etc.

Chairman.—How am I to justify this?

SRR.—In actual fact the work done by the library staff, other than one or two clerks, is all academic work: helping the readers, selecting books and papers from periodicals, to suit the needs of the readers, and organising the documents to make the service to readers pinpointed, exhaustive, and expeditious. In one of your letters you referred to the excellent work done by the staff of the Madras University Library. If you now recall its quality, you will grant that it was all academical and technical work.

Chairman.—Is there any precedent for such a recommendation?

SRR.—Oh yes, surely. You may remember the ugly politics in the University of Madras. Before the politics entered the University, it was possible for me to create most of the necessary posts and make recruitment on the basis of merit and competence. But after the ugly politics entered into the executive of the University, they began to transfer some clerks in the Registrar's Office to occupy any new place created or falling vacant in the Library with a slightly higher salary. I could not, in any way, resist this. You know the local reason for it.

Chairman.—This fact does not help me.

SRR.—You might remember that Mr Littlehailes became the Vice-Chancellor in 1934. As Director of Public Instruction he had seen the way in which the University Library had been treated. One day he told me, "You get all your unfulfilled plans and schemes put up in my period. You cannot get anything done after I go away." Among other things I mentioned my handicap in the matter of staff. He told me, "Show me a way to stop that bad practice." I suggested to him what I am now suggesting to you. He accepted it, and had it put through. It was easy for him because in those early years the Indian members of the Syndicate were rather afraid of Britishers and therefore his proposal was accepted without any opposition whatever. After the Syndicate Meeting Littlehailes rushed to my room and said, "Give your thanks to God. It has been put through. I was fully convinced with the various reasons contained in your note. This made me place the case before the Syndicate with firmness." I said, "No doubt, I thank God. But I should also thank you for having created a precedent in this country, for the other library authorities to follow."

Chairman.—I shall certainly follow that precedent.

SRR.—The moment your report comes out there will be a dog fight among the librarians of the several libraries of the Secretariat, as to who should be put in which scale. To avoid this I should like your report to include the classification of the library posts, or at least some principles to guide the classification.

Chairman.—That will be going too far. The terms of reference do not include it.

CHAPTER X

REPORT OF THE PAY COMMISSION AND AFTERMATH

1 Change of Yugas

We have a tradition about the junction of Kali-Yuga and the earlier Yuga. (A Yuga covers about 1,080,000 years). The junction of Kali-Yuga (the current Yuga) with its earlier Yuga occurred in 3102 B C. A case had been filed in a court of law a few days before the end of the earlier Yuga. The plaintiff A pleaded that B should be ordered to accept the repayment of a loan taken from him. But B said, "I did not give it as a loan. It was only a gift to help my friend. And so, I cannot take that amount back." The case was adjourned by two weeks. It was Kali-Yuga by that time. Now B demanded repayment of the loan. But A pleaded that it was a gift and not a loan, and therefore it is not repayable! Something like this happened in regard to Varadachary Pay Commission.

2 The Attitude of a Secretariat Librarian before the Report came out

Before the report of the Pay Commission was published, I joined the University of Delhi at the invitation of Sir Maurice Gwyer. Knowing about this, some of the librarians of the Secretariat came and asked me what I had recommended. As usual I respected the Canon of Reticence. Thinking that I had not made any recommendation, some shrewd librarians made week-end pilgrimages to my residence in the University of Delhi. One of them was a particularly smart man.

Smart librarian.—I hear that you have started to guide your library staff in research.

SRR.—Yes, I have.

Smart librarian.—Can you admit me to that research course?

SRR.—Certainly. I am only conducting the course in week-ends. You can easily come and join us.

Smart librarian.—On account of my poverty, I cannot afford to come in every week-end. I have to attend to so many odds and ends in the week-ends — in fact, also at the evenings of most of the working days — to make my family affairs run smoothly with as little difficulty as possible to any member.

SRR.—I can sympathise with you. Do as you please.

Smart librarian.—I gather that the Pay Commission has recommended for us a better scale by salary. As soon as it comes into effect, my family difficulties will disappear. I shall then become free to attend your research course, each week-end without fail.

SRR.—I wish you good luck.

3 Attitude of the Same Librarian after the Report came out

For several weeks after the Report of the Pay Commission had come out and the salary scale of librarians had been revised, this "smart young librarian" did not come to the University on any day. One evening I had to go to the Secretariat for a meeting. When I was within about two furlongs from the Secretariat, I saw the "smart librarian" coming towards me. He too seems to have seen me, and he turned to a narrow lane. Poor man, it was a little too late for him. I called him. He had the courtesy to come to me.

SRR.—How is it that you are not coming to the Research Meetings all these days?

Smart librarian.—What can I say Sir. When my salary was low I had one kind of family difficulty. Now that my salary has been doubled, another kind of family difficulty has come up.

SRR.—I hope that nobody has taken ill in your house.

Smart librarian.—No, Sir. Now that we have more money, all the members of my family insist on going for cinema as many evenings as possible, and certainly for the matinee on all the holidays. I feel helpless (Laughter).

4 During the Office Time

The higher status, taken to have come along with the higher salary, "entitled" the librarian to go as often as possible, to the Under Secretary or to the Deputy Secretary for a chat or for talking "Departmental politics." Thus, even the physical presence of a librarian in his library became more and more rare. But, whether he too did this or not, the librarian of the Ministry of Labour, unfortunately for him, started publishing a Documentation List periodically. His Minister, who was a voracious reader, appreciated this, and often sent for the librarian and got the benefit of his documentation service. This latter event reached the notice of the librarians of the other Ministries. This made some of them use their new status to go to the room of the Under Secretary of the Ministry of Labour, spend an hour or two in chatting and ejecting some venom into his mind against the Librarian of that Ministry. But that Librarian was not second to anybody else in putting the Under Secretary in good humour. However, the documentation list proved to be a real red-rag to the other librarians. The Librarian of the Ministry of Labour was regularly sending copies of his documentation list to the Chief Officers in the other Ministries. This made some of the Officers ask their respective librarians to give similar service. This was too much to bear after having become a gazetted officer.

Result: The Librarian of the Ministry of Labour was boycotted. No other Librarian of the Secretariat would speak to him.

5 Reaction on the Librarian of the Ministry of Labour

The Librarian of the Ministry of Labour did not mind this. He was capable of doing tit for tat. But through God's Grace, he abstained from doing so. On the other hand, the extra time gained by the excommunication, was turned on the intensification of his library service — in reclassifying the documents, in building up a depth version of Colon Classification for this purpose, and in giving intensive training to his staff in documentation work and service. He also produced special documentation lists on special occasions such as the Regional Conference of the International Labour Organisation held in Delhi.

CHAPTER y

FALSE PRETENCES: DEVELOPMENT

1 Classification of the Library Posts in the Secretariat

Each of the chief librarians of the Secretariat claimed the highest grade; on the ground that he was the head of his Library. The Finance Ministry disallowed it. Then the Home Ministry appointed a Committee to classify the posts of the chief librarians. It was decided that the classification should depend upon the number of volumes in the library. This gave an exercise to the ingenuity of some of the librarians. Without telling the librarians of other Ministries, some of the librarians quietly increased the number of volumes in their respective libraries. As a first step after that, they would ask for more book shelves and more space in the library. Then was to follow the request for their being upgraded on grounds of the number of volumes in the library. This false pretence came to my notice in one case.

2 Action of the Secretary for Economic Affairs

This happened in the case of a library, under the overall management of the Secretary for Economic Affairs. He was a smart I C S man. He could not be easily misled even by the smartest librarian.

3 My Advice Sought

The I C S Secretary felt that he should have expert advice in this matter. For this purpose, he sent his Deputy Secretary, an I A S man, to me.

Deputy Secretary.—My Secretary has asked me to get your advice about our Library.

SRR.—What is it about?

Deputy Secretary.—Our Librarian has sent in an application stating that,

1 The number of volumes in the Library has increased considerably;

2 More space and more shelves should be provided;

3 The number of volumes has reached the limit set for the upgrading of the chief librarian to the highest grade; and

4 He should be given that benefit.

SRR.—How can I give my opinions on this without quantitative data? More than data, I should base my advice on a first hand knowledge of your library.

Deputy Secretary.—Can you then come to our Library?

SRR.—I shall be glad to do so. You send me your office car.

Deputy Secretary.—I shall ask my librarian to bring the car to you.

Naturally the Deputy Secretary thought that it was but proper that his Librarian should be sent to collect me. But poor man, the cunningness of the Librarian was too deep for him.

4 The Trick of the Librarian

Two days later, the Librarian telephoned to Mr Das Gupta, the Delhi University Librarian, asking, "When will Professor Ranganathan be lecturing in the class?" Das Gupta said, "He meets his students between 12 noon and 1 p m, though he seldom lectures." One day, the Ministry's Librarian arrived at the University Library at 12-10. He told Mr Das Gupta, "Our Deputy Secretary has asked me to bring our office car here to take the Professor to the

Secretariat." Das Gupta said, "Nobody can go near him when he is in the class. Nobody can enter there. I won't do that." The Librarian said: "I had heard about it and I thought that he would make an exception in the case of a Government Secretary." Das Gupta reiterated, "No, no exception even if the President of India wants him!" "Thank you," said the Librarian. He then went back and reported to the Deputy Secretary, "Dr Ranganathan has refused to come." I did not know anything about it. Das Gupta came and told me after 1 p m, "So-and-so came here, I asked him to wait. He said that he could not wait, and went away."

5 Secretary Outwitted

Next day the Deputy Secretary himself came to me at about 3 p m.

Deputy Secretary.—Sir, Our Librarian reported that you declined to come.

SRR.—But you did not send your car.

Deputy Secretary.—Is it so? I sent it along with my Librarian.

SRR.—It is a story in itself. We shall not waste time over it.

Deputy Secretary.—To avoid such mishaps, I shall myself bring the car when I come.

SRR.—Come at 2 p m tomorrow.

He came at that time and I went along with him. When we entered the library, we found that the Librarian was not there.

Deputy Secretary.—What has happened to him?

The Library Assistant.—Sir, yesterday he left a leave letter with me, asking me to hand it over to the Office.

This morning I learnt that the Librarian has taken leave for two days with effect from today.

Deputy Secretary.—It does not matter. I shall myself take my friend round the library.

SRR.—May I pull out the volumes which are out of place in this Library?

Deputy Secretary.—Do as you please, Sir.

I examined the collection from one end to another. I found many old tattered books. There were as many as ten copies of the century old Adam Smith's *Wealth of nations*. There were also books without any relevance to the work of the Finance Ministry. The peon removed all such books and arranged them on the floor. The remaining books were all closed up in the shelves. As a result, half of the shelf space became vacant!

6 The So-Called Documentation List

The Library Assistant was watching all this. He did not understand what was happening. He suddenly remembered an instruction given to him by his Chief. He then brought a bunch of roneo copies. Each sheet had "Documentation List of the week" as heading. He gave the bunch to the Deputy Secretary. Then, we both went to the Secretary.

Secretary.—Is the documentation list all right?

SRR.—Where is the documentation list?

Secretary.—Here it is. Probably the Deputy Secretary did not show it to you.

SRR.—Good Heavens! This is not a documentation list. This is only a list of books added to the library from time to time and arranged in the sequence in which they are mentioned in the Book Seller's Bill.

Secretary.—What a fraud! I always suspected that something was wrong, whenever he brought the list to me and praised it to heavens.

Deputy Secretary.—I too could not discover this, Sir.

Secretary.—What about the extra-space required?

Deputy Secretary.—The Professor examined the volumes. They were mostly tattered copies of books published several years ago. For example, there were 10 copies of the century old Adam Smith's *Wealth of nations*. The Professor asked us to weed out all such books as they were of no use.

Secretary.—Has this been done?

Deputy Secretary.—It has been done. The Library Assistant has all along been telling me that his Chief took great pains to visit second-hand book sellers and buy those volumes at a cheap price.

Secretary.—Evidently there is no limit to his fraud. Ten copies of Adam Smith! Cheap price! What about the space problem now?

Deputy Secretary.—More than half of the existing shelves have become empty.

Secretary.—What about the total number of volumes, now?

Deputy Secretary.—It does not come anywhere near the minimum for the higher grade.

Secretary.—So, that problem is solved. Why don't you call him to me?

Deputy Secretary.—Knowing that the Professor is coming today, he has gone on leave for two days. When I sent him on the first occasion to bring the Professor, he came and told me that the Professor refused to come. Then I myself went. Then the Professor told me the story of the trick our librarian had played.

7 The Librarian Escapes

"The Goddess of Fortune is blind," they say. Sometimes fortune may favour frauds. Having had from his Assistant, a report of the happenings, the Librarian extended his leave through a letter sent from about a thousand miles away. During this period, the Secretary resigned his post, and the Deputy Secretary was transferred from Delhi. Hearing about all these from his Assistant, the librarian came back from his leave with a sense of triumph. He was indeed a pet of fortune. Was he not? We have a hypothesis known as Karma Theory, to explain "cause and effect" working in an unnatural way in the case of a person. According to this Theory he should have done something really good in his earlier birth to get fortune in this birth though he does not deserve it on the basis of the work done by him in this birth.

CHAPTER Z

LIBRARY STAFF OF NON-GOVERNMENTAL LIBRARIES

1 Library Staff of Universities and Colleges

11 ABSENCE OF THIS SPECIES OF LIBRARIANS TILL ABOUT HALF A CENTURY AGO

Since the foundation, in 1857, of the first three Universities in the Country — Bombay, Madras, and Calcutta — the British Government used the universities and the colleges only as tools to spot out the best intellects of the country and give them the necessary training for appointment in the lower positions in the Departments of the Governments. Universities were only Examining Bodies. In this set-up, teaching generally degenerated to filling up the memory of the students. This was not difficult because for about 60 years after the forming of the universities and the colleges, the students entering the colleges belonged to the uppermost centiles in the intellectual scale, and their self-educability was of a very high order. If some of them developed originality in thinking, and a few even did creative work, it was not due to the teachers or to the methods of teaching; indeed it was in spite of them. Further, examination became the be-all and end-all in that system, and examination was little more than testing the memory of the candidates. Above all, hardly any university or college had a functioning library, though some of them had small collections of gifted books locked up somewhere out of the way. Therefore, neither the universities nor the colleges had libraries or library service of any value till about 1911. But in 1911 the universities received special grants during the Durbar held in Delhi by the Emperor George V after his Coronation in London. Some of the universities used part of this special grant for starting a library. Thus there was in the country hardly any university or college librarian of a professional stature and giving professional service either to the teacher or to the taught till about 1915.

12 PROFESSOR AS HONORARY LIBRARIAN

By about 1915 some gift books had accumulated in some universities and colleges. The ritual respect for books needed their being looked after. But, the method of teaching inherited from the earlier century had not given any place for library work in the educational process. However, if an adventurous student or teacher wished to have the use of any book, it was not denied. This made it necessary to have a stock register for books. Thus came the need for some clerical work and attendants' work in the library. Even in this nominal set-up of a library, need arose for some person to have charge of the overall management and supervision. For this purpose, his need was met without any cost by appointing a Professor as Honorary Librarian. In Madras, the University Library was put under the care of the Superintendent of the Museum, who was already the Honorary Librarian of the Connemara Public Library with which the University Library shared the building; this continued till 1925. I was the first professional librarian in the country to have charge of a University Library. I took up the charge from 1924 provisionally and from 1925 onwards on a permanent basis. But, as a result of some of the money received from the Government of India during the Delhi Durbar having been diverted towards library development, some of the university libraries began to appoint a few persons of more than clerical calibre, to work in the library. However, this species of honorary librarians persisted even as late as 1959. In that year, the University Grants Commission had asked me to conduct a Seminar for university and college librarians. In that Seminar I found a professor joining us as honorary librarian of his

University. In private conversation I used to call him "the last of the vanishing species." Of course, the discussion of library techniques in the Seminar had little meaning to him. Nor had he experienced or sensed the need for teaching work and library work being integrated.

2 Look at This Picture and That

21 Advantage of the Library Staff of the Government of India

It is the staff of the libraries in the Government of India that were the first to get a proper scale of salary. There were three reasons for this success of theirs:

1 Most of them were concentrated within one campus and were therefore able to act collectively in mutual consultation;

2 The non-library staff of the Government of India, behind the "throne" as it were, managed to have a Pay Commission set up for their benefit; and

3 Though the library staff was not very much thought of, they woke up in time and succeeded in using my services to get their position being properly considered by the Pay Commission.

22 Disadvantage of the Library Staff of Universities and Colleges

The value of university and college libraries in the educational system is being slowly realised during the last half a century. Moreover with the establishment of a School of Library Science in Madras in 1929, systematic professional training is being given to the aspirants for posts in university and college libraries. Their number had certainly become larger than that of the librarians of the Government of India. But they had some handicaps:

1 The library staff of the university libraries were distributed among a number of autonomous universities; with the conseqence that

2 They could not act collectively;

3 The condition of college librarians was even worse, as some of them work in Government colleges and others in private colleges;

4 The Pay Commission appointed by Governments did not take them into their purview; and

5 The Inter University Board, which might have taken up their cause, did not at all do so.

3 U G C's Voluntary Help to the Library Staff of Universities and Colleges

31 C D Deshmukh and Myself: Contact One

Dr C D Deshmukh had become the Chairman of the U G C (= University Grants Commission) by 1 Feb 1957, when I came back to India from Zurich. Sometime after this when the Chairman of the U G C was expected to be in the Annamalai University, its Vice-chancellor took me to his University for help in matters concerning its library. One day after lunch in the Vice-chancellor's house, Dr Deshmukh and myself had a long conversation.

CDD.—We are now giving to each university library a substantial Book Grant — between rupees 100,000 and 200,000.

SRR.—I am glad to know about it. Evidently this must have happened during the three years of my absence from the country.

CDD.—In my visits to universities, I find that the Book Grant is not properly utilized. Heaps of books, containing multiple copies of one and the same book, are lying not brought into use.

SRR.—When does a university hear about the Book Grant?

CDD.—In December or January.

SRR.—Our book market is in London and in New York. Careful book selection and purchase from any of those markets is not possible within three or four months. But, the Grant should be utilized before the end of the next March — that is, within a period of three or four months. Therefore, the University librarian goes to Bombay, Calcutta, and Madras and buys whatever is available. In order to spend the Grant fully, he buys multiple copies of many books. This is cause one.

CDD.—What else?

SRR.—To process books worth more that Rs 100,000 and to bring them into active use, there should be adequate staff — classifiers, cataloguers, and documentalists.

CDD.—Will not the libraries have them already?

SRR.—The staff they have consists only of those found necessary for the poor book fund — in most universities less than Rs 20,000 — which they had before the U G C Grant came into vogue.

CDD.—But no Vice-chancellor of any university told me about this.

SRR.—The Vice-chancellor would not have found out even what you have found out. But, on grounds of prestige he would have merely ordered that the librarian should not allow even a rupee of the Grant to lapse.

CDD.—Not even any librarian told me about this.

SRR.—The librarian would not dare to. For, he would be afraid that his explanation could be interpreted to mean that he was incompetent.

CDD.—This is very strange. Why should they not have picked up courage?

SRR.—They could not, because most of them are poorly paid, and their words would not be heeded to by the Vice-chancellor or even by the Registrar. They would have naturally thought similarly about yourself.

CDD.—You mean to say that university people — Vice-chancellor and librarian — do not behave like the *Rishis* of Dandakaranya! Neither prestige nor poverty nor fear prevented them from showing to Sri Rama the bones of the *Rishis* killed by *Rakshasas* and asking for help.

SRR.—Exactly so.

32 C D Deshmukh and Myself: Contact Two

A few weeks later C D Deshmukh and myself met in Madras. This was, at his request, to discuss the ways and means of preventing the Book Grant, made by U G C, failing to serve its purpose and to take up the question of the salary of the library staff of universities and colleges.

33 Library Committee of the U G C

The discussion spread over a few days and it resulted in his inviting me to chair a Committee. It was asked to go into all the problems of university and college libraries in their entirety and make concrete proposals on the basis of which the U G C can formulate its policy. This was accepted. This Committee was appointed before the end of 1957. It held its first meeting on 19 Feb 1958 and its last meeting was held on 14 Feb 1959. A follow-up Seminar of university and college librarians was held from 4 to 7 March 1959.

34 INTERIM REPORT ON SCALE OF SALARY

Chapter J of the Report of the Committee was turned on the Salary and Status of the Library Staff of the Universities and Colleges. The substance of this Chapter was sent to the U G C as an interim report, some months before the full report was sent.

4 Press Copy of the Report of the Committee of the U G C

At the end of May 1959, I had to leave for U S A and Poland to attend International Conferences in Cleveland and Warsaw, and also to observe the working of the Viniti (National Documentation Centre, U S S R). Therefore, before leaving India I drafted the Report of the Committee and of the Seminar, made the press copy of the same, and sent it to the Secretary of the U G C. But, for some unknown reason, the Report was published in 1965 only.

5 Library Staff of University Libraries

51 RECOMMENDATIONS OF THE U G C

The following is an extract on the subject from the Report of the Committee of the U G C:

"J51 Designation, Qualification, Salary Scale

The following structure of the library staff, their functional designation, their professional status, their qualifications, their grades in a university library, and the corresponding scales of salary for each grade, are recommended. The salary scale should be changed to coincide with that of the teaching staff, whenever the latter is changed.

1	2	3	4		5	6
S N	Designation	Profes-sional Status	Qualifications		Grade	Scale of Pay
			Minimum (i)	Desirable (ii)		
1	Librarian	Profes-sional Senior	M Lib Sc II Class or MA or MSc II Class and Dip Lib Sc or B Lib Sc I class; A pres-cribed minimum experience in a re-search or a university library.	Doctorate in Library Science or any other subject.	1	800-50-1250 (Profes-sor's
2	Docu-mentalist	-do-	-do-	-do-	2	500-25-800 (Reader's)
3	Deputy/or Assistant Librarian	-do-	-do-	-do-	-do-	-do-
4	Reference Librarian	-do-	-do	-do-	-do-	-do-
5	Chief Clas-sifier	-do-	-do-	-do-	-do-	-do-
6	Chief Cata-loguer	-do-	-do-	-do-	-do-	-do-
7	Maintenance Librarian	Profes-sional Junior	Dip Lib Sc or B Lib Sc I class and B A or B Sc or B Com II Class		3	250-20-500 (Lecturer's)

1	2	3	4		5	6
SN	Designation	Profes-sional Status	Qualifications		Grade	Scale of Pay
			Minimum (i)	Desirable (ii)		
8	Assistant Classifier	Same as for Maintenance Librarian				
9	Assistant Cataloguer		-do-	-do-		
10	Accession Librarian		-do-	-do-		
11	Periodicals Librarian		-do-	-do-		
12	Circulation Librarian		-do-	-do-		
13	Senior Library Assistant in any Section but not the Reference Sec	Profes-sional Assistant	-do-	-do-	4	150-10-250 (Assistant Lecturer's)
14	Junior Library Assistant in any Section but not the Reference Sec	Semi-Profes-sional	Cer Lib Sc and good Higher Secon-dary Certi-ficate		5	80-5-150-10-220

"J52 Apprentice Course

A person without previous experience as a member of library staff should have certified apprentice service for six months in an approved library to become eligible for any of the posts mentioned in Sec J51.

"J53 Transitory Measure

A person already in service in a library without the prescribed or equivalent qualifications may be put in the grade just below the one recommended for the place to which he is assigned. As and when each such person leaves the service, his post should be brought in conformity with the prescription in Sec J51.

"J54 Absence of Qualified Person

As a transitional measure for about five years or till a person of prescribed or equivalent qualification becomes available, a librarian may be appointed in grade 2. During that period the Deputy or Assistant Librarian and the others assigned to grade 2 may be appointed in grade 3.

"K4 Data for Strength of Library Staff

The strength of the staff for the different sections is to be determined roughly on the following basis:

1 Book Section:—One person for every 6,000 volumes added in a year.

2 Periodical Publications Section:—One person for every 500 current periodicals taken.

3 Documentation Section:—One person for every 1,000 entries prepared in a year.

4 Technical Section:—One person for every 2,000 volumes added in a year.

5 Reference Section:—One person for every 50 readers (other than the users of the text-book collection) in a day.

6 Circulation Section:—One person for every 1,500 hours for which one wicket gate of the library has to be kept open in a year.

7 Maintenance Section:—One person for every 6,000 volumes added in a year, one person for every 500 volumes to be replaced in a day, and one person for every 100,000 volumes in the library.

8 Administrative Section:—Minimum of one library accountant, one steno-typist and one correspondence clerk.

9 Supervisory Section:—One Librarian and one Assistant or Deputy Librarian.

10 Unskilled staff:—One cleaner for every 30,000 volumes in the library; one attendant each for every 6,000 volumes added in a year, for every 500 current periodicals taken, and for each of the shifts in the Circulation Section, besides unskilled and the semi-skilled workers normal to any institution."

52 Implementation of the Recommendation of the U G C

The U G C treated the recommendation, of the Library Committee about the scale of salary, as an interim report (*See* Sec z34). Along with the recommendation of the revised scale of salary for the library staff, the U G C had also agreed to share with the universities the extra cost needed for the purpose. In spite of it, it took several years for many of the universities to implement the scale of salary recommended.

53 A Temporary Fall in Standard of Service

Now that the scale of salary and the status have been raised to the desired level, all expect that the library staff of the universities live up to their full stature and give the best documentation service to professors and students. But, unfortunately reports reach me from the general readers, professors and occasionally even from a few Vice-Chancellors that the service in some of the university libraries has deteriorated instead of improving. It is sad to hear this. I have myself seen a University Library which used to throng with readers from 4 to 7 p m till about 1950, having not more than two readers (!) when I happened to visit that Library at about 6 p m one day in 1963. However, I used to plead with those making complaints that service will improve in about a few years as and when an abler set of persons are attracted by the new scale of salary to work in university libraries.

54 Appeal

The library staff of the universities should dedicate themselves to their work. In Renascent India their work plays a vital part in the building up of our Nation. The stimulus given by a proper and adequate documentation service to professors and research scholars should be able to give them. a momentum which will carry them through their research work all through life. It is again the library service given to the university students that will fit them to become informed, intelligent, and helpful in the development of our industries, in the cultivation of our human resources and in the functioning of democratic Governments in our country. My appeal to the staff of the university libraries is that they should function up in the best way possible.

6 Scale of Salary Recommended for the Library Staff of Colleges

61 U G C's Recommendation

The following is an extract from the Report of the Committee of the U G C on the scale of salary for the Library Staff of Colleges:

"J61 Large College Library

In a large college with an annual book fund of not less that Rs 20,000 the librarian should be in grade 2 with qualifications appropriate to it.

"J62 Small College Library

In a small college with an annual book fund of less than Rs 20,000 the librarian should be in grade 3 with the qualifications appropriate to it.

"J63 Other Staff in a College Library

The other Staff in a college library should be in grades 3, 4, and 5 or grades 4 and 5 as the case may be with qualifications appropriate to them.

"J64 Transitory Measure

A person already in service in a college library without the prescribed or equivalent qualifications may be put in the grade just below the one recommended for the place to which he is assigned. As and when each such person leaves the service, his post should be brought in conformity with the prescriptions in sections 1, 2, and 3."

62 RESTORATION AFTER A TEMPORARY SET-BACK

The recommendation, "The salary scale should be changed to coincide with that of the teaching staff, whenever the latter is changed," mentioned is Sec J51 of the *Report* of the Committee (*See* Sec z5) is applicable to the library staff of colleges also. But, when the Government of India transferred the subject of college librarians from the U G C to the Governments in the Constituent States, this recommendation was lost sight of; with the result that the scale of salary of college librarians went below that of Demonstrators and Instructors in Physical Education. Fortunately by their own enterprise, the Associations of the College Librarians of some of the Constituent States have set this matter right. It is hoped that this will soon happen in all the other Constituent States.

7 Library Staff of Research Institutions

The recommendations of the Pay Commission of the Government of India and of the U G C have virtually come into vogue in most of the research libraries — be it in industries or in research institutions. In a Meeting of the Advisory Committee of the Insdoc, the Director General of the C S I R (Council of Scientific and Industrial Research) mentioned that he had secured a revised scale of salary for the Scientists of the C S I R family of laboratories. When I asked him whether he had secured for the library staff the revised scale of salary he said that he had forgotten about it. However, he had the ready wit to tell me in effect, "I shall declare the library staff under the C S I R to be scientists. That would prove sufficient." He actually did so.

8 Library Staff of the Public Library System

The four Constituent States — Tamil Nadu, Andhra Pradesh, Karnataka, and Maharashtra — have a statutory Public Library System. The librarians belonging to this group have not yet had the benefit of the recommendations of the Pay Commissions of the Government of India or of the U G C.

81 Situation in Tamil Nadu

The situation is at its worst in Tamil Nadu; with the result, only non-graduates with a three months' certificate course in library routine form most of the staff of its Public Library System. Only a very small number of graduates with a Degree in Library Science are found in the Staff of its Public Library System — not even one in many of the District Library Systems.

82 An Unsuccessful Attempt to Remove the Anomaly

In 1962, when Hon'ble Shri Baktavatsalam was the Chief Minister and the Minister for Education, I took up the problem with him. He took a memorandum from me. He also held a Conference of District Library Authorities to improve the scale of salary of the librarians among other things. At his invitation, I also attended the Conference. The Hon'ble Minister had to leave the Conference after his opening speech and my speech, leaving the Conference to the care of the Director of Public Instruction, the *ex-officio* Director of Public Libraries. My recommendation was not at all brought to the notice of the Conference. I am looking forward to the day when this mistake would be rectified in Tamil Nadu. I also hear that the Government of Tamil Nadu is likely to remove this unfortunate anomaly.

83 Situation in Andhra Pradesh

The position is said to be slightly better in Andhra Pradesh. But it has not yet reached the recommended standard. I hope that this will soon be attended to by the Government of the Andhra Pradesh.

84 Situation in Karnataka

In Mysore State the Public Libraries Act came into force in 1965. At the request of the Government as a follow-up of the Act, I had furnished it with some suggestions and Rules on the scale of salary of the staff of its Public Library System. But this has not yet been implemented. On the other hand, it is learnt that the Secretariat is collecting information about the scale of salary prevailing in the Public Library System of Tamil Nadu. This method of looking around for the lowest scale of salary available anywhere in the country and adopting it in violation of the latest ideas and practices and expert recommendations is an unfortunate habit. I trust that when the Ministry is set up this wrong method will be given up and that the staff of the Public Library System of the Karnataka State will be put on a scale of salary indicated by what is in vogue in all the other Library Systems in the country.

CHAPTER A

INTERNATIONAL ORGANISATION FOR DOCUMENTATION

1 International Institute of Bibliography

Even as early as 1895, Henry La Fontaine and Paul Otlet of Belgium realised the need for minutely classifying papers in periodicals and other micro documents. This implied a sense for the feeding of specialists with micro documents — with nascent micro documents. A world accumulation of 12 million documents, consisting of books and papers in periodicals — macro documents and micro documents! Annual rate of increase is a hundred thousand books and a million papers! How to keep track of this ever swelling flood? How to keep every intellectual worker fed exhaustively and expeditiously with just the documents relevant to the work engaging his thought at the moment? This was the challenge. To consider this, an International Bibliographical Conference was held in Brussels in 1895. The outcome was the founding of the International Institute of Bibliography. The Government of Belgium provided the funds for it.

2 International Federation for Documentation (F I D)

In 1931, the International Institute of Bibliography was renamed as International Institute of Documentation. This was the first time that the term 'Documentation' replaced the term 'Bibliography'. In 1938, its name was again changed to International Federation for Documentation (F I D). And the Headquarters was moved from Brussels to The Hague. Donker Duyvis had been its Secretary-General even from 1924. He continued to hold that office till his death in July 1961.

3 Composition of the F I D

The F I D consists mostly of specialists in diverse subjects — particularly industrial research workers. To my knowledge, it did not have an appreciable number of librarians till about 20 years ago. No doubt they promoted the publication of documentation lists on several subjects. But the majority of the members have been persisting in regarding U D C as its prestige possession and in perpetuating its use in documentation work. Unfortunately, none of them had any notion that library classification was itself a specialised discipline to be left to the care of a specialist in that field.

4 Role of Donker Duyvis in Respect of Library Classification

Donker Duyvis was the first to recognise that U D C could not be adapted to the modern needs of documentation, by make-shifts such as "Starving Digits." He was the first to realise that the revision of U D C should be based on a Science of Library Classification. I had not known anything about him. But in 1947, I was agreeably surprised by an invitation sent by him to give my views on the "Place of Classification in Documentation." A few months earlier than that I had joined the University of Delhi. In response to this, I wrote my paper *Classification and international documentation*, and sent him three copies of it — one for himself, one for circulation among friends in U K, and the third for similar use in U S A. But, he wrote back saying in effect: "This paper could not be disposed of in that way. Have you any objection to my printing it?". I had certainly no objection. He then published it in a whole issue — pages 154 to 177 — of the *Review of documentation*, 14, 1947. He also arranged, through Unesco and the British Council, for my attending the F I D Conference, held in The Hague from 17 to 19 June 1948. The precirculation of this paper appears to have roused some curiosity in some of the members of the F I D. For, I was asked to address them on Faceted Classification. The audience was only about 20 — not even a fifth of the members attending the Conference. Miss Ditmas of U K told me that it was the first time that at least a few of the specialist research workers forming the F I D ever attended any meeting on Classification.

5 Committee on General Theory of Classification (F I D/C A)

In addition to having created this opportunity for the F I D members to become aware of the distinct discipline of the science of classification, Donker Duyvis also managed to establish the F I D/C A in 1950, with me as Rapporteur-General. I continued to hold this Office till 1962, when this Committee ceased to exist. Each year I used to furnish a report on the progress made in the theory of library classification. In 1957, the F I D brought about the first International Conference on Classification. It was held in Dorking, near London. My address was on "Classification as a discipline." This Conference was largely attended by librarians and it emphasised the need for a faceted scheme for classification to meet the requirements of documentation. In 1961, we failed to communicate the results to the F I D. The F I D/C A was abolished in 1961.

6 Committee on Classification Research (F I D/C R)

F I D/C R was formed as the successor of F I D/C A. This Committee was entrusted to Denmark with Dr Rasmus Molgaard'H as its Chairman. The Committee nominated me as its Honorary Chairman. In 1964, this Committee convened the Second International Conference on Classification at Elsinore, Denmark. And I was invited to deliver the Opening Address. In this Conference I found, to my great delight, that about 50 per cent of the audience consisted of research workers and computer engineers, other than librarians. Their interest in classification had just then begun to develop. In fact a Norwegian Engineer attending the Conference took me to Oslo, to have further discussion on the subject.

7 Fight Continued

The prestige-owners of U D C, still dominating the F I D and not showing any interest in the science of library classification, have not yet accepted any recommendations of Conferences and Committees made of the classificationists. Till now, they have only accepted the Octave Device and the Packeted Notation. Professor Neelameghan told me that in the Yugoslavia Conference of 1971, just a few specialist research workers had begun to realise the essential role of the classificationist in documentation, in the design of depth classification, and in the improvement of U D C. Thus the gulf between the die-hard scientists in the F I D and the librarians is being bridged very slowly only. This is unfortunate. My faith is that the day will soon come when this gulf would be removed.

8 Unesco

Unesco came into existence as a specialised agency of the United Nations Organisation, shortly after World War II. Since its formation in 1946, its Division of Libraries has been doing its best to be a powerful ally of all the Laws of Library Science. It is exercising its influence on the production of international documentation lists — such as abstracts — so that overlapping of effort may be eliminated and no subject field is left uncovered. It is also wielding some influence over the international non-governmental bodies, such as the F I D and the I S O (International Standards Organisation) to promote some degree of international standardisation in Documentation. It gives them financial aid to carry out specified projects in documentation. As an international organisation, Unesco has been helping in the organisation of national documentation centres in several countries.

CHAPTER B

NATIONAL ORGANISATION FOR DOCUMENTATION

1 United States of America

The first country to sense the importance of Documentation in the progress of research and industries was U S A. As early as 1908, it established its Special Libraries Association to take charge of this problem. But unfortunately, in U S A also the gulf between Documentalists and Librarians has not yet been bridged. However, I may state here as an aside that during my visit to U S A in 1950, I found that Association had collected copies of all special schemes for the depth classification of many specialised subjects. Even then the vastness of the collection of special schemes was appreciable. It was this that made me feel that the depth classification needed for documentation should not be a special one designed for each depth subject, but that a universal scheme should be designed with the capability of being carried to any depth in any depth-subject whatever. This view, formed in 1950, has now brought us to the concept of "Freely Faceted Scheme for Classification." It is already giving good results. My belief is that it will give ever increasing results if it is pursued by continuing research, keeping step with new depth-formations in the universe of subjects.

2 United Kingdom

Perhaps U K was the second country to enter the field of documentation. For this purpose it founded in 1924, its Aslib (Association of Special Libraries and Information Bureaux). Here too the dominant members had been for long drawn from industries. The gulf between Documentalists and Librarians continued to be wide for a long time. In 1950, I made a humble attempt to bring the Aslib and the Library Association together. But there was resistance from the former. However, there is some improvement in the last few years. Aslib has begun to take librarians on its research staff. It is promoting Documentation Work and Documentation Service in U K.

3 USSR

31 Organisation of Viniti

During the third week of September 1959, I had the opportunity to visit U S S R. My focus of interest was its National Documentation Centre — denoted by the initio-nym "Viniti." It was established in 1952. I spent nearly a week in studying its working. The lady in charge of acquisition of periodicals was very efficient. I saw, in her collection, some Indian periodicals not known to me! What was more interesting was that, she gave me a list of Indian periodicals of which she could not get copies and she wanted my help!

32 Flow of Work

The Section of Documentation Work was equally interesting. Its organisation was efficient. The Classifying and Cataloguing staff had been divided into a few groups. Group 1 had only a few beginners. It made an entry of each paper in a process card, and added to it the Class Number of its Basic Subject. Group 2 marked a few further digits in the Class Number — corresponding to one facet of the subject, as we call it. The members of this Group had more experience in classification than those of Group 1. They were also slightly larger in number than Group 1. The slightly more detailed classification done by this Group needed this. In due course, each periodical along with a process card for each paper in it, reached the Group in charge of final classification. Its members were all experts in classification, and their number was greater than that of the earlier Group, as it should be. This team consisted of Classification specialists in different subjects. They entered in each process card the final Call Number of the concerned paper. They also inserted the class numbers and other data for cross reference entries, in the case of each multi-focal paper. Sometimes, a specialist passed the whole material to another specialist to enter the data about cross reference. Thereafter the team of cataloguers completed the work. Lastly, there is revision by a group of revisers. Thereafter, the documentation list is properly edited and passed on to the Publication Section.

33 Other Services

Another activity of the Viniti is called "Express Information". Sometimes this work is done on demand, and very often in anticipation. I was particularly interested in the Reaction Index provided in their Documentation List dealing with Chemistry. Viniti is also providing a considerable number of translations made by the appropriate translators picked out from the panel-list maintained by it. Viniti further provides "Signal Information Service" which gives a list of current titles in certain subject fields.

34 Friendship Established

During this visit, its Director, Academician A I Mikhailov, and his deputy Dr A I Chernyi became good friends of mine. Their friendship is of considerable professional value.

35 Other National Documentation Centres in USSR

Apart from Viniti, U S S R has also National Information Centres on certain special kinds of research work. These are:

1 All Union Institute for Medical and Medico-Technical Information;

2 All Union Institute for Scientific and Technical Information — Agriculture;

3 Central Institute for Patent Information and Techno Economic Research;

4 All Union Reserch Institute of Technical Information, Classification and Coding; and

5 Current Commercial Information Institute of Current Economics Research Institute.

4 Other Countries

After World War II, National Documentation Centres were organised in many countries. The following are some of these:

1947	Norway	1953	Uruguay
1948	Portugal	1954	Brazil
1949	Rumania	1956	Pakistan
1949	Yugoslavia	1957	China
1950	Mexico	1957	Hungary
1950	Poland	1957	Japan
1952	India	1957	Philippines
1952	Turkey	1960	Argentina

5 Special Kinds of Documents

A national documentation centre should include in the documentation list not only published documents but also unpublished Doctoral Theses and Research Reports of industrial houses, so far as they are available for public use. If necessary, these lists may each form into a documentation periodical of its own, independent of a documentation periodical for published papers.

CHAPTER C

BEGINNING OF DOCUMENTATION SERVICE IN INDIA

1 First Documentation Service in India: Raman Effect

From July 1925 to July 1928, I was busy in organising the Madras University Library along helpful lines. During that period undergraduates formed the largest group of readers visiting the Library. Therefore, my service to the readers was only that of a "Librarian on floor duty". In this work, I associated with Shri C Sundaram who was one of the early recruits to the library staff as a raw graduate. By 1928, he had picked up the right library spirit. In March 1928, Sir C V Raman had discovered "New Radiation". Later in that year, the University of Madras invited him to deliver the "Sir Subramanya Iyer Lectures" for the year. The subject announced by him was "Properties of Liquids". A few hours before the Lecture, he called at the University Library. I gathered from him that his main theme was the "Application of his New Radiation to the study of Properties of Liquids". Immediately after he left, Sundaram and myself decided that we should use the opportunity to do good documentation service in the nascent ideas on the subject of Raman's Lecture. This made us make a thorough search of all the periodicals, current in our Library, in Physics and in General Science, from March to that day, to find out papers on the subject. This yielded about 60 papers — micro documents — on the New Radiation. The paper in the Fortnightly Report of the French Academy of Sciences had denoted the new Radiation by the term 'Raman Effect'. Therefore our Documentation List carried in its title the term 'Raman Effect'. Roneo copies were made immediately. We inserted a book mark in each volume at the proper place where the documented paper began. We then arranged the volumes in our

"Topical sequence book rack" and put at the top of it the Guide "Raman Effect"! Copies of this documentation list were distributed to the members of the audience that evening as an appetiser to make them to come to the Library and take our documentation service. Raman himself was pleased with this enterprise of the Madras University Library and particularly with the term 'Raman Effect' used in the title of the List. Both after the lecture on that very day and during the next few days, several members of the audience came to the Library and looked through the papers. Perhaps this was the first attempt in India in doing documentation service with nascent micro documents on a very specialised subject.

2 Documentation Service to Generalist Readers

The joy derived in doing the documentation service on Raman Effect made us attempt similar service from time to time. As research had not put on steam in Madras in those early years, our service was largely turned on generalist readers. At the time of the Centenary of any scientist, we used to publish in the Dailies of Madras a documentation list on his works. The concerned volumes were displayed as was done in the case of Raman Effect. This brought an appreciable number of readers to the Library to make use of the documentation service. On such occasions our documentalists did intensive documentation service. We did similarly, on all important national and international days and on the annual festival days of India.

3 Advance Documentation Service

31 Before 1936

Professors and post-graduate students gradually found joy in looking up the periodicals and studying the deep papers found in them. In addition to the vague desire for research, this experience attracted them towards research in about two or three years. By that time, it was possible for me to get five smart young fresh graduates, appointed as documentalists. Getting this staff sanctioned was facilitated, to a large extent, by some of the professors that had experienced the benefit of documentation service from 1928 onwards. Some non-university, non-English-knowing scholars also showed the desire to have the benefit of documentation service. They were, therefore, admitted as special members of the Library.

32 Documentation Service in Two Popular Subjects

Sensing the possible demand for micro documents from parts of books — particularly from the popular subjects in English Literature and in Education — we had been giving profuse cross reference entries — that is, subject analyticals — in the Catalogue. These entries were of great help in doing documentation service to scholars in full satisfaction of Law 4 of Library Science — Save the time of the reader. News about this service appears to have reached some other parts of India; as a result almost every month from about 1936 onwards we used to receive requests for similar documentation service from scholars, particularly Ph D candidates, from as far as Kashmir in the North to as far as Travancore in the South. I remember a lecturer in Kashmir asking for such a help for his Ph D Thesis on Galsworthy. Such requests increased the enthusiasm of our documentalists.

33 Documentation Service in Natural Sciences

By 1936, about half a dozen scientists had begun to do systematic research in Madras. Their subjects of pursuit were found out from them. In those years, the foreign mail used to come at about 7 a m every Saturday. About 200 or 300 periodicals used to come on that day. These were quickly processed. Immediately thereafter, I used to peruse quickly the periodicals in the subject in which some research was in progress in Madras City. After the persual, a letter was sent to each of the known research scholars giving a list of the papers relevant to his work found in the periodicals received. In the case of one or two persons information was sent through telephone. This service was continued till about 1942. By that time World War II had prevented the regular receipt of periodicals. About the same time, other adverse local factors also led to the muffling of the enthusiasm of the documentalists.

4 Documentation Service to the Veteran Vijayaraghavachariyar

Salem Vijayaraghavachariyar was one of the prominent leaders of India in those years. He was the President of the Meeting of the Indian National Congress held at Nagpur in 1920. In 1929, he wrote to me whether I could give him some information about the earliest migration of Hindus to U S A. We had hardly any material in our Library on the subject. Therefore, I sought the help of the Library of Congress, U S A. Within about six months, that Library sent me a long documentation list on the subject. I found only one of the items as a paper in a volume in our Library. I sent a copy of the list to Vijayaraghavachariyar and also the one volume. It was about 10 a m early in 1930. Vijayaraghavachariyar, though an Octogenarian, walked into my library. I had never seen him before that. I felt greatly honoured. He returned the volume to me.

SRR. In this old age, you need not have taken the trouble to come all the way from Salem. The book could have been sent by post.

Vijayaraghavachariyar.—No, no. I could not resist the desire to thank you personally for the magnificent list you have sent me.

Then he marked some of the items in the list as of special interest to him. I then got those items on inter-library loan from the Library of Congress. Years later, in 1958, I happened to go to Salem. Knowing that I was in the town, one of the young men of his family met me. He told me that in their family, the service the Madras University Library did in 1929 to the Patriarch of his family was often remembered and talked about; and that old gentleman used to mention it to his family and to his friends quite often. This is a testimony of the kind of joy awaiting a librarian doing documentation service in all earnestness and thoroughness.

5 Documentation Service to His Holiness Sri Sankaracharyar

In 1932, His Holiness Sri Sankaracharyar of Kamakoti Peet was camping in Madras. One day he told me, "I conjecture that when our people migrated to U S A, long long ago, they had built some temples there. One of them was a Ganesha temple. Can you find some evidence for it?" The documentation list received from the Library of Congress for the use of Salem Vijayaraghavachariyar contained many titles published or distributed by the Smithsonian Institution of Washington. I had already got copies of some of them. These volumes were carefully searched by our documentalists. They found a near-picture of Ganesha in one of the volumes, and there was also a short write-up. Sankaracharyar felt very pleased to find that his conjecture had turned out to be true.

6 Documentation Service to Dr C Rajagopalachariar

From 1937 to 1939, Dr C Rajagopalachariar (now 94 years old) was the Chief Minister of Madras. Early in 1938, he had accepted the invitation to deliver the valedictary address of the Mathematics Association of the Presidency College, Madras. He telephoned to me that he wanted a copy of Pott's *Algebra* which he had studied while at college. We did not have a copy of it. I told him that I would give him some substitute book if I could know the information he wanted. He mentioned, "History of Indian Mathematics". I said that I had more than a dozen books carrying information on the subject. He said, "Send me one or two books" and also added, "Can you also send me a list of all the books?" We quickly prepared a list showing the pages of each book in which Indian Mathematics was treated. Anticipating that he might mention to the audience the fact of our having several books on the History of Indian Mathematics, we pulled out all the volumes mentioned in the list, inserted book marks at the proper places and put them on display in our topical sequence and put up to the top of the book rack the guide card "Rajagopalachari's Lecture on Indian Mathematics". Our conjecture was right. From 5-30 p m that evening, students came to the Library one after another. Some more came on the next few days. We had the pleasure of doing precise documentation service to these students. This shows that a documentation list prepared for one reader may be of use to many others.

7 Documentation Service to Sri Aurobindo

In 1940, a messenger came from Sri Aurobindo, the well known sage of India, living in Pondicherry. The sage wished to have the exact location of the passage. "*Brahma Satyam*

Jagan-mithyā" (= The Absolute Exists; the World is an Illusion). The Advaitic ring of the passage made us search for it in Sankara's Works. But these were in 20 volumes and they had no index! As we could not fail to do the necessary documentation service to such a great soul, three of us began to examine each quarter of every verse. As we were going through volume two, we got an unexpected help. Sri T Sundarachariyar, an old advocate in my home town, Shiyali, stepped into my room. He was a "walking concordance" to many of the classics in Sanskrit. In ten minutes, he located the passage. The documentalists in us felt relieved. We were also delighted to have done documentation service to such an eminent sage. This experience emphasises that we should provide indexes to our classics, whether individual or collected. There are many cases needing this attention. The library profession of India should take up this work as quickly as possible.

8 Experience of Other Libraries in India

I have experience of the beginnings of documentation service in the Madras University Library only. In those far off years, the University libraries in Bombay, Calcutta, and Lucknow were the only other libraries with facilities and resources, for documentation work and service. But, I have no knowledge of their experience of the beginnings of documentation. I wish that somebody collects and publishes a reliable account of outstanding concrete cases of the early documentation work and service done till about 1940 in those and any other libraries.

CHAPTER D

BEGINNINGS OF DOCUMENTATION WORK IN INDIA

1 Forest Research Institute, Dehra Dun

11 Amateurish Ledger System

The credit of having started a systematic continued large scale documentation work, for the first time in India, goes to the Forest Research Institute, Dehra Dun. It was only for the use of its own staff. This work was done in an amateurish way by the heads of the different Departments of research. To classify the documents, a special scheme was designed. It is said to have become the basis for the "Oxford System of Decimal Classification for Forestry"

12 Recommendation by the One-man Commission

In 1947, at the suggestion of Sir Maurice Gwyer, I was invited as a One-man Commission to make suggestions for the improvement in the documentation work of the Forest Research Institute. The chief points in my report were:—

1 The research personnel making the documentation "ledgers", implied wasting the research potential of the Institute;

2 Moreover they cannot afford to learn the latest techniques of documentation work;

3 The documentation techniques form a discipline by themselves; and they are ever growing; and

4 The proper method would be to entrust this work to the library and appoint as its librarian, a person with a good training in documentation work and service.

This recommendation was accepted. Eventually Mr K A Issac, B Sc, M Lib Sc, one of my students in Delhi, was appointed as its first Documentalist.

2 National Institute of Sciences

The credit of producing the first abstracting documentation periodical in India, goes to the National Institute of Sciences. This had the title *Indian science abstracts*. It was started in 1935. First, it covered only papers published in India. Later on, it also included papers of Indian origin, irrespective of the country of publication. Due to lack of adequate support, this publication could be continued only up to 1940. Actually, even in 1960, the Working Party of Scientists, appointed by the Planning Commission, found that it would be uneconomical to revive the *Indian science abstracts*; and the Planning Commission approved this.

3 Central Board of Irrigation

The year 1936 is another important epoch in the early history of documentation work in India. During this year, the Central Board of Irrigation started its abstracting periodical entitled *Quarterly bulletin*. If I remember right, this was due to the enterprise of Mr Montagu, an Officer of the Central Board. Though he was not a documentalist by profession, as a consumer of documentation he had realised the value of documentation. This abstracting periodical has been continued as the *Irrigation abstracts* published by the Central Water and Power Commission. These abstracts were prepared by engineers, specially assigned to this work. All the observations made about the agency for documentation work in Dehra Dun are applicable here also.

4 Medical Periodicals

The provision of abstracts for medical documents has been looked after by a number of Indian medical periodicals. Each of them sets apart a section of each of its issues to this work. This should have been due to the realisation of the non-viability of a separate Medical Abstracting Periodical for the papers published in India.

5 Industrial Bibliography

During World War II, there was an urgent need for developing Indian industries. As a preliminary step, a survey was made of the existing arrangements for documentation work, in each of the industries. The result of this survey was published as *Bibliography of industrial publications in India.* This was virtually a select documentation list. Then followed the Council of Scientific and Industrial Research (1942). One of the first activities of this Council was the compilation of a dictionary of economic products. For the use of this compilation, several publications were scanned and a short summary of each economic product was posted on a sheet of paper called "Ledger sheet". However, these were not shaped into a systematic documentation list, available to others.

CHAPTER E

PRESENT DAY ORGANISATION FOR DOCUMENTATION IN INDIA

1 Documentation Research and Training Centre (DRTC)

The functions of the DRTC are to,

1 Do research in documentation techniques, continuously refining and sharpening them;

2 Train students for advanced documentation work and service;

3 Give refresher courses on the subjects to the practising documentalists;

4 Train students and other documentalists in the preparation of the depth version of the Colon Classification for the classification of micro documents going with one or other basic subject; and

5 Train students and other documentalists in doing research in the techniques of documentation work and service.

2 Indian Standards Institution

The functioning of the Documentation Sectional Committee and of the Library Building and Furniture Sectional Committee of the Indian Standards Institution are to establish standards for,

1 Techniques involved in Documentation such as Library Classification and Library Cataloguing;

2 Make-up of certain relevant parts of books and periodicals such as Preliminary pages, Bibliography, and Index;

3 Presentation of the text in a book or in a paper;

4 Abstracts — both indicative and informative.

5 The stages in doing Documentation Service; and

6 Physical aids needed in Documentation Work such as apparatus and equipment.

3 Service Library

The Fuctions of a Service Library are to,

1 Periodically contact each specialist reader of the parent institution — either in his work place or elsewhere — and find out from him his exact documentation requirements;

2 Receive from each specialist reader his requisition for his exact documentation requirement;

3 Make and circulate periodically a Local Documentation List, tailored to the exact needs of the specialist readers of the library and in particular of the research workers in its parent body;

4 Receive and circulate, to each specialist in the parent institution, the issue of the National Documentation Periodical prepared by the National Documentation Centre, as and when it is received;

5 Get the necessary help from the National Documentation Centre in the preparation of a Documentation List, needed by a specialist of the parent institution, if a complete list is beyond the capacity of the local resources;

6 Get from the National Documentation Centre reprographs and translations of papers needed for local use, if their preparation is beyond the capacity of the local resources; and

7 Give intimate personal service to each reader (*See* Sec 14).

4 Indian National Scientific Documentation Centre (Insdoc)

The Functions of the Insdoc are to,

1 Acquire by air mail, a microfilm copy of the contents page of the issue, being currently produced, of each of the periodicals taken in the country, in its subject field. If it is too costly,

2 Acquire by air mail, a proof copy of the contents page instead of a microfilm copy of it;

3 Make a classified catalogue of the papers in the contents pages, with a direct or indirect bearing on the research work in progress in the country;

4 Print periodically — Say, once in a fortnight or once in a month — and send out copies of the classified catalogue, mentioned in category 3, to each of the participating specialist and other libraries in the country; so that

5 The classified catalogue reaches the participating libraries before or on the same day as the full issues covered by it reach them;

6 Preparation and keeping up-to-date, of a documentation list of the Doctoral Thesis in the Natural Sciences, approved by the Indian Universities;

7 Supply, on request, to any service library a 'documentation list on the subject specified by it and also certified by it as being beyond its local resources;

8 Procure or make, on request for any participating library, a reprograph of any particular paper not available locally but needed by its clientele;

9 Procure the reprograph even from a foreign library, if the original is not available within the country;

10 Arrange for the supply, on request to any participating library, a translation of any paper needed by its clientele; and to facilitate this work,

11 Maintain in cards, an ever-up-to-date Union Catalogue of the holdings of the periodicals in Natural Sciences in the different libraries in the country; for,

111 Facilitating its translation work; or

112 Advising the requesting library about the location of the original paper to be translated in a library near to the requesting library, in case it has a translator in its own locality or neighbourhood.

12 Publications of a biennial list of Natural Science Periodicals currently taken in India;

13 Publish the National Union Catalogue of Periodical Publications in Natural Sciences at suitable intervals, to enable any participating library to locate by itself the nearest library from which it can borrow any volume of any periodical;

14 Maintain in cards information about the subjects in which research is in progress among the clientele of the participating libraries.

5 Indian National Social Science Documentation Centre (Insodoc)

The Functions of the Insodoc are to be similar to those of the Insdoc.

6 Indian National Documantation Center for Humannites

There should be an Indian National Documentation Centre for Humanities — Mysticism and Spiritual Experience, Fine arts, Literature, Linguistics, Religion, Philosophy, and Psychology.

7 Indian Association of Special Libraries and Information Centres (Iaslic)

The Functions of the Iaslic are to,

1 Make contact with the research workers in the specialist and other libraries in the country, and make them documentation conscious;

2 Make contact with the industrial and other business houses, research institutions, and the Departments of Governments, and persuade them to have libraries of their own doing documentation work and service; and

3 Maintain in cards a Directory of specialist libraries in the country, showing against each library its having or not having a documentation wing;

4 Inform any isolated research worker, not attached to any institution, about the facilities available in the country, for getting help in documentation service, on receipt of an enquiry from him; and make it known widely that the Iaslic can do this service; and

5 Coordinate the functions and the work taken up by the several documentation organisations in the country, so as to ensure the fulfilment of the principles laid down in Sec E7.

8 Out of Bound for a Documentation Centre

The responsibility for the maintenance of a dormitory collection or of a copy right collection or of a service collection of books, periodical publications, and other kindred reading materials should not be assigned to any organisation for documentation work — such as the Insdoc and the Insodoc. this work should be totally left to the care of the respective National or State Libraries. This applies equally to maintenance of a collection of Doctoral Theses. This should be left to the care of the respective Universities. If any document, including a Thesis, is needed by a Documentation Centre for reprograph or translation purpose, it can be borrowed by the Documentation Centre. This will be facilitated, if a National Documentation Centre is located in close proximity to the National Library in the concerned subject. It is not desirable even to house it in the same building as the National Library concerned. For, the functional designs for a Service Library and for a Documentation Centre have to be quite different.

91 Coordination and Cooperation

There should be a holistic coordination and cooperation in work among the organisations for National Documentation, mentioned in Sec E1 to E7 and the different National Libraries. Here, emphasis should be put on National Service Libraries, as there is a tendency to forget the difference in function between a Library and a Documentation Centre. No organisation should encroach upon the function of any other. Each should act strictly within the sphere assigned to it and totally avoid taking up any of the functions of any of the other organisations. This, it should do in the full confidence, that every other organisation will be doing its best in the sphere assigned to it. If any one of the organisations swerves away from this holistic principle or is negligent of its work, the forum provided by the Iaslic should be used to remove any such defect. Having the seven different organisations and the National dormitory library, National copyright library, and the National Service Libraries — each with its own assigned and distinctive functions — is helpful. This helpfulness should not be lost by lack of coordination and cooperation. Otherwise the stigma of "Too many cooks spoil the broth" will descend upon the system. Nor is it wise to ignore the dangers implied in Parkinson's Law and to assign all the functions or even more than one function to one and the same organisation.

CHAPTER F

DOCUMENTATION RESEARCH AND TRAINING CENTRE

1 Genesis

11 Analysis of the Requirements for Industrialisation

The foundation of the DRTC was due to the statesman scientist Professor P C Mahalanobis F R S, Founder and Director of the Indian Statistical Institute. As a member of the Planning Commission in charge of Pespective Planning, he had to think ahead. While doing so, he was convinced that:

1 the Development and the well-being India depended upon its industrialisation;

2 Industrialisation could not make satisfactory progress unless it was based on industrial research and the pure research needed to back it;

3 Our industries would lag behind those of other countries, if the industrialisation is based mostly on imported results of research and know-hows — particularly because most of them would be outmoded by the time of our picking them up; therefore,

4 New know-hows should be discovered and designed by research in our own country;

5 The research potential of the country would be dissipated unless research is done on Relay Principle;

6 To make our research workers do their very best, the Relay Principle should include not only the work being done in India but also that being done in every other country;

7 Our research potential can be conserved and made to yield the maximum results, if and only if prompt, exhaus-

tive, and pin-pointed documentation service is given to our research workers. And as a necessary means for it,

8 Documentation work in anticipation as well as on demand is done in the country by a National Documentation Centre and by each Service Library; for this purpose,

9 There should be intensive training of our documentalists; and

10 There should be continuous research in improving and refining the theory and techniques of documentation work and service.

12 Contact 1 with Professor Mahalanobis

When Prof Mahalanobis had reached this conclusion, he seems to have thought of me. Hearing that I had left the country and getting my Zurich address, he met me during his very next visit to Europe. It was in 1956. He invited me to come back to India and take charge of research and training in documentation. But from my experience of India till 1955, particularly with Insdoc, I felt that our industrialisation was lagging far too behind to accept and benefit by documentation. But he pleaded that:

1 Industries were coming up and becoming aware of documentation needs faster than expected;

2 He had heard that, in the past, the latest techniques of documentation were being designed in India under my guidance; and

3 I should not shirk my responsibility to do my best to our country at this important time.

13 Contact 2 with Professor Mahalanobis

My having migrated to Europe in 1954 and my return back to India in 1957 were due to the following reasons:

1 I wished to improve my own work on documentation by associating myself with the industrially advanced countries of Europe; for this purpose,

2 I had migrated to Europe and was planning to stay on there; but,

3 The foreign exchange regulation of our country stood in the way of drawing my pension outside India; and therefore, I had to come back to India.

I reached home on 1 February 1957. Sometime after it, Prof Mahalanobis invited my wife and myself to Calcutta, to show me the facilities available in the Indian Statistical Institute for conducting a Documentation School. In this second contact in Calcutta also I repeated my old argument that our industries had not developed sufficient awareness on the problems mentioned in Sec F11. I therefore stated that it was then premature to start a Documentation School in India. Apart from this my wife said that she would like to continue to be in South India, unless we could go back to Europe. This meant that even when the time would come for Documentation School being established, and if I should conduct it, it should be in Bangalore; because, we were settling down in that city.

14 Period of In-Action

In Zurich, documentalists of different countries used to come to me for the study of documentation techniques, each for two or three months at a time, according to an agreed programme. This gave me that necessary stimulus for research in documentation. I could also visit the industries where my documentation technique was applied and assess its efficiency or otherwise. But there was no such stimulus in Bangalore. Nor was there any professional atmosphere to provide colleagues in the profession, with whom I could continue the research in documentation done by me in Zurich. Therefore the five years from February 1957 to April 1962 turned out to be virtually a period of painful in-action for me.

15 Contact 3 with Professor Mahalanobis

In 1961, a few industries wrote to me wishing to have the benefit of documentation. This led me to feel that the twilight of industrialisation in all earnestness was beginning in our country. In the middle of 1961, Shri J Saha, the Librarian of the Indian Statistical Institute, and then the major domo, so to speak, of Prof Mahalanobis, happened to meet me in Delhi. He renewed the suggestion of Prof Mahalanobis and asked for a memorandum on the subject. The memorandum was sent to Prof Mahalanobis within two weeks after that. It received the approval of Prof Mahalanobis and also the sanction of the authorities of the Indian Statistical Institute. It was said to have received the concurrence of the Prime Minister Pandit Jawaharlal Nehru. Prof Mahalanobis further stated that the Indian Statistical Institute was contemplating on a fairly big Centre in the South and that the Documentation School might be located in Bangalore as part of that Scheme.

16 DRTC Becomes a Fact

I was asked to look for a rented building for the School. Fortunately, within two days I heard that a suitable building within 200 yards from my house, was about to be rented to the Posts and Telegraph Department for storage purposes. I immediately contacted the Mysore Government and had the building released for Documentation School. But within two days I had to leave for Europe to attend an International Conference on Cataloguing in Paris, and the Ter-Centenary of the German National Library in Berlin. Therefore, I wrote to Calcutta to send some responsible person to Bangalore, for completing the negotiation and taking over the house. When I returned home about a month later, I found that everything had been done. Prof Mahalanobis had also requested Shri Srinagabhushana, Head of the Statistical Quality Control Unit, Bangalore, to be the Special Officer of DRTC and to take charge of the entire administrative work, so that I could concentrate my attention totally on academic work. Shri Srinagabhushana was of immense help. It was decided to denote the contemplated School by the name "Documentation Research and Training Centre" — short name "DRTC." Such was the genesis of DRTC.

2 Delay in Starting Work

21 The Inevitable Delay in Getting Things Ready

The building was occupied on 1 January 1962. It took about two months to get the necessary furniture and other equipment. About March that year, Shri Banerji, a member of the staff of the Library of the Indian Statistical Institute, was sent over from Calcutta to be one of the teachers. Shri A Neelameghan, a very able, industrious, and well informed documentalist, offered to join the staff. He had to his credit excellent documentation service done to the members of the Hindustan Antibiotics Ltd, Pimpri, for some years. He joined in April. They two as salaried teachers and myself as honorary professor spent a few weeks in finalising the syllabus, the method of training to be adopted, and the topics on which research should be undertaken in the first instance. We were ready to begin regular work from 1 June 1962.

22 Delay in the Insdoc Sending Its Deputed Candidates

In my scheme for the improvement of the Insdoc furnished to the Planning Commission in 1959 (*See* Sec H38 and its subdivisions), I had stated that the Insdoc was not able to get trained documentalists for its work, on account of no University School of Library Science in India paying sufficient attention to this subject. This subject was only one of the several optional subjects for the M Lib Sc Course organised by me in the University of Delhi in 1948 at the request of Sir Maurice Gwyer, the Vice-Chancellor, till my leaving that University in 1955. Therefore I had stated in my scheme that the Insdoc itself should run a Documentation School, as it was not done by any other agency. But, as soon as the establishment of DRTC was made firm, Prof M S Thacker, the Director-General of CSIR and the ultimate Head of the Insdoc, enquired about the DRTC and whether it was still necessary for the Insdoc staff to take up the training of documentalists. According to him, taking up the responsibility for conducting a School of Documentation would adversely interfere with the legitimate work of the Insdoc. I told him that it was not necessary. We agreed that DRTC should give preference to the candidates deputed by the Insdoc and by the CSIR (Council of Scientific and Industrial Research) in general. For the first year, five seats were reserved for them. It was also agreed that the Insdoc itself should give to the candidates a two months' course of apprenticeship and orientation and send them to DRTC in June 1962. But the names of the candidates were not received by D R T C till the beginning of June. Nor did we hear of any Orintation Course being given by the Insdoc.

23 Chance Removal of the Delay

Early in June, Prof M S Thacker and myself happened to fly together from Delhi to Bangalore. He enquired about DRTC. I had to tell him that the work could not be started, as the Insdoc had not sent the five candidates to take the five places reserved for them. He felt disappointed.

On the next day, he called at the DRTC and sent an urgent telegram to the Head of the Insdoc to send the candidates immediately. The candidates joined after the middle of June; but as the Insdoc had not given them the Orientation Course, the DRTC itself had to give it for a few weeks. This delayed the beginning of the regular training. Moreover, of the five candidates, one had a few years of experience in the Insdoc and had attempted to get one of the teaching posts in the DRTC; it was difficult to understand why he was selected. Another candidate withdrew herself from the Course.

3 Plan of Work

31 Teaching and Research Inseparable

At the higher reaches, research work and training of specialists should not be separated. Without active research by the staff, teaching cannot lift the students to a high level of thinking; nor can it fill them with enthusiasm and faith in the social benefit of library service in general, and of documentation service in particular. Without the opportunity of teaching advanced students, the fountain of research will not become sufficiently profuse. The organisation of the work in DRTC is based on this assumption. Further, documentation is concerned with the happenings in the wave-front of knowledge taking shape in the hands of research workers. Therefore, new situations will arise in documentation from time to time. To meet such situations the documentalist of an institution should himself be able to do some development research. To make a student fit for this, he has to be given some training and exercise in doing research in documentation.

32 Intimate Teacher-Student Contact

The class is engaged as a whole by the teacher only

for about three hours a day. At other hours, the students do their daily assignments individually. Thereafter they meet one teacher or another in small groups or even individually for tutorial work and for taking the help of any other kind.

33 DRTC: A Residential Istitution

The DRTC has been made a residential institution. The teachers themselves live either within the campus or within about 500 yards from the DRTC. This arrangement provides facility for any student meeting any teacher during the whole day, for the library of the Centre being used at any hour of the day, and for team research.

4 Inauguration of DRTC

41 Message from Prime Minister and Others

After the completion of the Orientation Course, the regular work of the DRTC was inaugurated on 18 August 1962 by Dr C D Deshmukh, the President of the Indian Statistical Institute, and Chairman of the University Grants Commission. The Hon'ble Justice Sri Nittoor Sreenivasa Rau, Chief Justice of the Mysore State, was in the Chair. The inauguration began with a message from Pandit Jawaharlal Nehru, the Prime Minister of India, reading as follows:

"India has made considerable advances in the technique of documentation. It is right, therefore, that we should have a Research and Training Centre and invite people from abroad to it also".

Professor A Neelameghan read out also messages from the Governors of the Constituent States, and from the International Federation for Documentation, Institute of Scientific Information of the Academy of Sciences of USSR, Belgian Association for Documentation, Brazilian Institute for Bibliography and Documentation; from the Library of the World Health Organisation, the Library of Congress (Washington), the British Museum Library, and the German State Library (East Berlin). About 200 scientists attended the function.

42 Dr Deshmukh's Address

Dr Deshmukh inaugurated the Centre with the following words:

"The Report of the UGC Committee brought out by Dr Ranganathan will guide the development of university libraries for at least a generation. The formation of this particular Centre is due to the informed enthusiasm which has been such a characteristic of Dr Ranganathan's career, and it is a happy coincidence that this enthusiasm has been matched by the understanding of those who are responsible for running the Indian Statistical Institute. Documentation is a natural extension of the use of the printed word and that use is not confined only to books; the real stuff and substance of research work appears today in scientific periodicals. If one does not keep abreast of them, then one is putting oneself out of gear. Even though research work will continue to be an individual effort, no research worker can any longer work in his own cubicle. There is no doubt that undefinable element of fortune, accident, intuition, or flash of imagination without which a hypothesis does not get born. But that flash will come all the quicker if the research worker knows exactly what is being done by others. After all, much of the fundamental research has to be done in universities. The universities, I should think, will benefit from the work that will be carried on at this Centre."

5 Methods of Training

51 Systematisation by the End of 1965

It was only after the first three years, that a suitable third Member of the teaching staff could be appointed on a long term basis. Indeed we could not find a competent teacher till one of our own alumni would have gained experience. This was made possible only in December 1965. I was waiting till a suitable teacher could be found, to withdraw myself from the regular work in DRTC. I wanted to do it, because it was improper for an old man of my age to stand between young men and their opportunities. But I had agreed to keep myself in close touch with the research activities of the DRTC. By that time, we had nearly systematised the methods of training.

52 Essential Features in the Method of Training

The following are the essential features of the method of training in DRTC:

1 One way talk and dictation of notes are avoided;

2 On each subject, there may be only one or two lectures at the beginning of the Course on it to present the highways and byways of the subject;

3 There may also be one or two lectures at the end of the Course on that subject to summarise all the points covered in the Course and to indicate areas for further study and for developmental research after the Course is over; and

4 The chief methods of communication between the students are Discussion, Tutorial, Project work, Case study, Weekly colloquium, and two Annual Seminars.

6 Performance

61 Absorption of the Alumni in the Profession

From 1962 to 1971, 59 persons were trained in DRTC. Of these 56 earned the award of "Associateship in Documentation". Of these 46 are now in positions carrying a salary of over Rupees 400 and more upto 1,250. Five have gone abroad. The remaining 5 have just started in a scale of Rs 210 to 425. These belong to the latest two years.

The above summary shows that appreciation of the value of the service of documentalists is just beginning. In the earlier years, the DRTC Alumni reported that they were handicapped by the "Associateship in Documentation" of the DRTC being regarded by the Public Service Commission as below the standard of M Lib Sc. This made me send to the Government of India showing in parallel columns the contents of the curricula for M Lib Sc and for the Associateship in Documentation. Nothing was heard for some months. When I was in Delhi early in 1967, I heard that some interested persons were responsible for the trouble. Then, I telephoned about this to the Officer concerned in the Government of India. He said that he had sent my statement to the Inter University Board for evaluation and advice, and that he had not received any reply from its Secretary. On his telephoning to the Secretary, he got the reply that on the advice of a senior librarian, a Committee of three members had been appointed to consider the matter (It was found that none of the three had ever taken the M Lib Sc course or taught it. Two of them had not conducted even the B Lib Sc course). And yet, the Secretary of the Inter University Board further added that the Committee had advised him that the Standard of the "Associateship in Documentation" of the DRTC was lower than that of M Lib Sc. The Officer of the Government told him that a perusal of the tabular statement forwarded to him should have convinced him that the reality was just the opposite. He further added that the Government would be obliged to turn down the expert advice of the Inter University Board if its Secretary simply forwarded to the Government, the adverse advice of the "so called" Expert Committee, without his own observation on it. Then the Secretary appears to have woken up. Ultimately the Home Ministry accepted the recommendations of the Public Service Commission that the two degrees were nearly of the same standard, but that the holder of an "Associateship in Documentation" should be preferred to an M Lib Sc, for posts of documentalists. Thus the correct decision of the Government in the matter was due to sheer chance. A theist would attribute it to the Grace of God.

62 Visiting Research Scholars

DRTC provides facility for research scholars and senior librarians to come and stay in its campus for short periods of two or three months or even longer, to work on specific projects. Since 1966, eight documentalists have taken advantage of this facility.

63 Learned Media Being Published

DRTC is pulishing proceedings of each of its two Annual Seminars. It collaborates with the Sarada Ranganathan Endowment for Library Science in the publication of the quarterly *Library science with a slant to documentation,* started in 1964.

64 Contributions by the Teachers and the Alumni of DRTC (up to 1971)

The total literary output of the teachers and the alumni of the DRTC during the first nine years numbered 624. The following table gives an analytical list of them.

Contributors	Books	Paper				Total
		Total	Research papers	Technical report	Depth schedule	
Teachers	8	469	438	5	26	477
Alumni	–	147	84	–	63	147
Total	8	616	522	5	89	624

7 Some Suggestions for the Future

71 ACCOMMODATION

The DRTC has outgrown the capacity of the present rented campus. This may soon introduce many undesirable elements. Moreover, it stands in the way of admitting foreign students. Therefore, the parent bod of DRTC should erect the necessary buildings. For this purpose an extensive site has already been acquired, at a nearly nominal price from the Government of Mysore, in the Mysore Road, Bangalore. This site is adjacent to the site earmarked for the Bangalore University. The cooperation between these two bodies will be mutually profitable. In the new building there should be the following provisions:

1 The main building should provide for lecture rooms, demonstration rooms, exhibition rooms, and a room for each teacher to enable him to hold the tutorial classes and small group discussions in his room;

2 Accommodation for the library designed in the most functional manner, as part of the main building. There should also be a Conference room. These two may be shared in common with the other departments of the Indian Statistical Institute located in the Campus;

3 Quarters for all the members of the staff including the servants;

4 A hostel building with all the modern amenities, providing a separate living room for each of the regular students, and for each of the visiting documentalists coming to DRTC for a limited period to do a specific piece of work under the guidance of the teachers;

5 A guest house with at least three rooms to accommodate visiting lecturers; and

6 Provision for water supply, electricity, and other amenties drawn from the municipal supply with certain precautionary measures, such as overhead tank for water. These will be shared in common with the other departments of the Indian Statistical Institute located in the campus.

72 Getting the Cooperation of Industries and Research Institutions

At present, some effort is being made to convince the industries and the research institutions in the country about the value of having specialist libraries of their own and manning them with documentalists, and for this purpose deputing candidates for training in DRTC. It is slowly bearing fruit. Ways and means should be found to enlarge this effort.

73 Increasing the Admission to DRTC

As the industries realise the importance of the training in DRTC, need will arise to increase the admission. But this should not result in large classes inevitably leading to mass teaching in the place of the large amount of individual attention and instruction now so effectively and purposefully practised. This will also result in lessening the research effort. The plan should be to open more units of the present size of teachers and students. Each unit will continue to work as the existing unit does. But all the units should share in common activities such as Weekly Colloquia and Annual Seminars.

74 Same Campus and a Single Head

It goes without saying that all the units, including the entire staff and students, should be in the same campus with intimate relation with one another under a single head.

75 Follow-Up Work

Necessity will arise to take steps to place the alumni in appropriate places, and to follow their career closely with full interest. There should be intensification of,

1 The present practice of keeping in close intellectual relation with the Alumni;

2 Stimulating them to engage themselves in some piece of research work or other germane to or arising from their own subject of specialisation; and

3 Providing opportunity for exchange of their results through the Annual Seminars, Periodicals, and other publications.

76 Consultant Service

A small squad of Consultant-Documentalists should be maintained by DRTC. The DRTC should send them to particular industries and other agencies in the country, to give them consultant service. This will require a very careful planning, so that the cost of the consultant is made up entirely of the consultant fee collected.

77 Report of the Work Done by the Alumni in the Year

It will be helpful if each of the Alumni gives a report to the December Seminar of each year, a detailed account of the most exacting case of documentation service done by him during the year.

8 A Potential Danger to be Watched Against

The success of the work of the DRTC will depend on the intimate cooperation of the members of the staff, in research as well as in teaching. They should form a team with mutual accommodation and understanding and free from tension of any kind. But, it is difficult for this to happen, if the number in the Team exceeds three. Then the intellectual interest making them to work as one soul in many bodies may be corroded by the ego-centred emotions, inherited by humanity from the earlier forms of evolution. Once this happens, other troubles will intensify it. Life tenure with a salary scale comparable to that obtaining in the country in most professions, may make the staff to settle down to routine teaching and to avoid doing research. This may also be induced by the overbearing nature of the Head. This is essentially a human problem peculiar to research and advanced training in documentation. It is equally true in any department of a University engaged in research and advanced teaching. There are many instances of a department of a university falling a victim to such a happening. When such a thing happens on account of the strength of the staff exceeding a small limit, we reach the end of the tether as it were. The incidence of such situations can be prevented only by the Grace of God. The Grace of God can be got by prayer. I conclude this Chapter with the fervent prayer that the DRTC should be Blessed by Him to continue as a nest of singing birds — forming a mutually respecting team of workers.

CHAPTER G

INDIAN STANDARDS INSTITUTION: DOCUMENTATION SECTION

1 Genesis

The genesis of the Documentation Section of the Indian Standards Institution has been described in Sec f1 and f2. I was Chairman of the Documentation Section from 1947 till the beginning of 1967.

2 Performance

At the instance of its Documentation Sectional Committee and of the Library Building and Furniture Sectional Committee, the Indian Standards Institution has published 23 Standards between 1947 and 1971. Of these 16 are directly or indirectly relevant to Documentation Work. The following is a list of them:

IS:2550–1963	Glossary of classification terms. 1964.
IS:796–1966	Glossary of cataloguing terms. 1959; 1966
IS:790–1956	General structure of preliminary pages of a book. 1956
IS:791–1956	Half-title-leaf of a book. 1956
IS:792–1964	Title-page and back of a title-page of a book. 1956;1964
IS:794–1956	Practice for table of contents. 1956
IS:4–1963	Guide for layout of learned periodicals. 1949;1963
IS:2381–1963	Recommendations for bibliographical reference. 1963
IS:18–1970	Guide for abbreviations of words in titles of periodicals using Roman alphabet. 1971
IS:1275–1958	Rules for making alphabetical indexes. 1959

IS:382–1952 Practice for alphabetical arrangement. 1952

IS:795–1956 Canons for making abstracts. 1956

IS:1250–1958 Proof corrections for printers and authors. 1958

IS:3083–1966 Code of practice for the procesing of microfilms. 1966

IS:3130–1965 Code of practice for storage and use of microfilms of permanent value. 1965

IS:1829 (Part I)–1961 Library furniture and fittings: Part I Timber. 1961

Note.—

1 In the specification mentioned as the last item in the above list, the following are likely to be of use in Documentation Work:

1 Catalogue Card Tray and Cabinet
2 Classifier's Table
3 Cataloguer's Table
4 Catalogue Cards Work Tray
5 Catalogue Cards Box

2 There is also need for the following:

1 Standard 125mm×75mm cataloguing slips
2 Standard 125mm×75mm cataloguing cards
3 Duplicating equipment

CHAPTER H

SERVICE LIBRARY IN INDIA

1 Definition

11 DISTINCTION OF SERVICE LIBRARY FROM DORMITORY AND COPYRIGHT LIBRARIES

1 Dormitory Library.—It preserves for the occasional use by posterity a representative copy of each of the documents produced or received in the country at any time, but no longer much in demand. Such a library will be ever growing.

2 Copy-right library.—It preserves one copy of each of the documents published in the country for legal purposes and as a permanent exhibit of the intellectual output of the country, but seldom given out to readers, because copies of these books will be available for use, either in the Dormitory Library or in the Service Library. A copyright library will be ever growing.

3 Service Library.—It is a compact library of documents expounding current ideas and in current demand and use by readers. It will weed out periodically the documents either worn out by use or outmoded in idea and release for disposal in consultation with the national and/or state dormitory library, as the case may be. The number of volumes in it will not grow beyond a certain limit determined by the kind of the library.

12 KINDS OF SERVICE LIBRARIES

There should be plenty of Service Libraries. The following five kinds of Service Libraries may be recognised:

1 One Public Library in each locality within walking distance from the house of any of its residents, normally giving general service to each generalist reader;

2 One Academic Library within the campus of a University, a College, a School, as the case may be, giving generalist or specialist service to each member of its parent body according to his needs;

3 One Specialist Library in each of the other kinds of institutions — such as an industry, a research organisation, a commercial house, and a Governmental Department — giving documentation and other forms of service to each member of its parent body;

4 One National Service Library in a small country; and

5 One National Service Library and in addition one State Service Library in each Constituent State in a large country.

13 Period for Weeding Out

The following periods for weeding out are suggested in a Service Library:

1 In a local generalist library — Public Library — any volume including that of a periodical publication may be weeded out after it has been kept for use for a period of 30 years. However, if a volume of a classic of permanent value continues to be in good condition, it should not be weeded out. But this should not happen if the library had been actually carrying out the demand of Law 3 of Library Science — Every Book its Reader. For, in that case, the volume would have been worn out by use and would call for being weeded out on this ground. Further, if the volume is of permanent value, a new edition would have come and a copy of it should replace the worn out copy;

2 In a University Library or in a Specialist Library, a volume of a periodical publication may be weeded out after they have been kept for use for a period of 60 years, unless an earlier weeding out is indicated in any particu-

lar case or no weeding out is desirable on account of its unusual frequency in demand;

3 In a National or State Service Library, no volume in sound condition (not worn-out by use) whether a book or of a periodical publication should be weeded out until it has been kept for use for a period of 60 years. It is only after that period, that a volume should be weeded out and released for disposal in consultation with the National and in addition the State Dormitory Library in a large country.

14 MAINTAINING AUTHORITY

The maintaining authority of a library will vary with the kind of library.

1 The maintaining authority for a Public Library, will be its local library authority, usually created by legislation, and in the case of an independent privately owned public library, the maintaining authority will be the person or the committee owning it;

2 The maintaining authority for any Academic Library will be its parent academic body;

3 The maintaining authority for any Specialist Library will be its parent institution;

4 The maintaining authority for a National Dormitory Library or a National Copyright Library, and a State Dormitory Library or a State Copyright Library will be the National and State Government, as the case may be;

5 The maintaining authority for a National Service Library and for a State Service Library will respectively be the National Government and the State Government.

15 NATIONAL SERVICE LIBRARY-SYSTEM

As a result of a higher rate of annual production of documents in each country and in the world as a whole, and of an increasing specialisation in the subject of interest to readers, there is a world trend to replace a single National Service Library by a System of National Service Libraries. The formation of a separate National Dormitory Library and a National Copyright Library has been already mentioned in Sec G12. The formation of a separate National Service Library for each of the major subject groups such as Natural Sciences and their applications, Humanities, and Social Sciences has already begun even in some of the Western countries with long library tradition of having a single omnibus National Library — such as U K and U S A. Among the Natural Sciences, a trend has also begun to have further specialisation, such as Pure Natural Sciences, Engineering and Technology and other Applied Sciences such as Agricultural Sciences, and Medical Sciences. The trend towards further specialisation has not yet begun in Humanities, and in Social Sciences. Perhaps, it may begin in the Social Sciences any time within about 25 or 30 years.

16 Application to India

The National Library of India was started with the name Imperial Library in 1902. It has been continuing all along as an omnibus library. But it has already become too large in stock as well as in staff for efficient management and rendering of service. Many of its volumes are not much in demand. There is also the Copyright collection. The volumes in current use get virtually "occulted" by the enormous number of volumes in the Dormitory and the Copyright collections included in the library as if they all formed a single collection. The usual difficulties of increase in the size of the staff is already being experienced. The time has come to replace the single omnibus National library by,

1 A National Dormitory Library;

2 A National Copyright library; and

3 A system of National Service Libraries along the lines indicated in Sec G15.

A separate National Service Library for each of the

1 Natural Sciences (other than Agriculture and Medicine)

2 Agricultural Sciences; and

3 Medical Sciences;

is already in an incipient form. A scheme has already been sanctioned and brought into force for the formation of a National Library for Social Sciences. If these are formed and the relevant books are transferred to these from the existing omnibus National Library, the residue in that library will form the National Service Library for Humanities. The coordination of the system of National Service Libraries will have to be in the hands of a Committee of the National Service Library System. It should consist of the chief librarians of the different National Service Libraries with the Union Minister for Education as its Chairman. The Secretaryship of the Committee may be rotated on an annual basis among the chief librarians. The Secretary for the year will represent the library system of India in all international affairs concerned with libraries.

2 Growing Number of Service Libraries

Documentation Service, whether to a generalist or to a specialist reader, should be essentially of a personal nature. This service can be effective only if it is based on a trilogue between

1 the Documentalist;

2 the Specialist reader;

3 the Documents in the stack room and their catalogue cards (*See* Sec h4).

This is particularly so in the case of specialised documentation service. Therefore, it is possible only in a Service Library — Local or University or National Service or State Service Library. Documentation service, the *summum bonum* of all library work, is fully realised only in a service library. The number of Service Libraries giving specialised documentation service to specialist readers is now appreciable and is steadily growing.

3 Increasing Appreciation of the Value of Specialised Documentation Work and Service

The beginnings of specialised documentation work and service happened in India only about half a century ago. (*See* Chap C and D). Since a few years after our Independence, the appreciation of the value — even the necessity — of specialised documentation work and service, has been growing. The new generation of librarians are developing enthusiasm for such a service. This is seen in the change visible — since 1963 — in the participation of the librarians attending the Annual Seminar of the DRTC. Till about 1965, the older librarians used the Seminar largely as an occasion for a holiday trip to Bangalore and its neighbouring places of importance. Few of them did more than attend the opening session and put in attendance on one or two days of the week. This has been a continuation of what generally happened in the Indian Library Conferences till 1963. From 1949, I arranged in the Biennial All India Library Conferences, a serious seminar-like discussion of the Papers circulated in advance. But this was disliked by most of the librarians. They went away for sight-seeing. Only very few, other than the authors of the papers, stayed back to participate in the discussion. But now the total absorption of the younger generation of librarians in the work in the DRTC Seminars is praiseworthy.

4 An Example of the Unexpected Potentiality of the Younger Generation

During the Annual Seminar of 1968, I had a reassuring experience. A batch of three librarians from Upper India happened to call on me on the second day of the Seminar. They were evidently under the grip of the old tradition.

Visitors.—We are glad that we got this opportunity to visit South India and to see some of its temples, and their architecture.

SRR.—When do you go for sight-seeing?

Visitors.—Tomorrow morning, Sir.

SRR.—I am sure that you attended the Group Meetings of this afternoon and the Lecture of yesterday evening. Did you find them interesting?

Visitors.—They were awfully interesting.

SRR.—Then why should you not stay for three more days, take an active part in the discussions in the Seminar and postpone your visit to after the last day?

Visitors.—(After looking at one another) We think that we can do so, Sir. It did not strike us.

These three librarians of Upper India called on me again in the evening of the last day of the Seminar.

SRR.—I am glad that you stayed on for the whole Seminar. Do you leave for sight-seeing tomorrow or this very evening?

Visitors.—No Sir, we have abandoned that idea!

SRR.—Why such a change?

Visitors.—Till now, the Conferences attended by us were all holiday affairs. In this Seminar we were greatly impressed by the absorption of most of the participants in the work of the Seminar from morning to evening, day after day. We have learned what a joy it is to be totally absorbed in our work for about eight hours each day. This makes us continue our exchange of ideas even after the official hours of the Seminar — during our walk and at the dinner table.

SRR.—I am glad to hear about this. But this need not prevent you from taking a trip for sight-seeing for a couple of days.

Visitors.—No Sir. We do not want to lose even a fraction of the new attitude towards our work, developed in us during the Seminar. Sight-seeing will dissipate that attitude. We wish to go back home immediately and start documentation work and service in our libraries and also throw ourselves wholly into the work of our library.

SRR.—May God Bless you.

I saw in them Free Renascent India! This shows the unexpressed potentiality in our young librarians to do and enjoy intimate documentation service to readers, and also to give their thought and energy to their library work in full measure.

5 Performance: Documentation Work

Since 1960, about 60 documentation lists are being brought out regularly by the service libraries. Of these, the following lists are produced by specialist libraries in which either the alumni of DRTC or the persons that have worked in DRTC for two to three months are working as documentalists:

1 *Desidoc list* (Fortnightly) Documentation group, Science Information Bureau, Metcalf House

2 *Title service for current scientific literature* (Bimonthly), Research and Development Establishment (Engineers)

3 *Technical abstracts* (Monthly), Research and Development (Engineers), Poona

4 *Bibliography of current titles* (Fortnightly), Space Science and Technology Centre;

5 *Bibliography of scientific and technical reports* (Bimonthly), Space Science and Technology Centre

6 *Highway documentation* (Fortnightly), Central Road Research Institute

7 *D E R L Documentation list with indicate abstracts* (Weekly), Defence Electronics Research Laboratory, Hyderabad

8 *E R D E documentation list* (Fortnightly), Electronics and Radar Development Establishment

9 *Weekly title service* (L R D E) Electronic and Radar Development Establishment

10 *NALSDOC* list (Monthly), National Aeronautical Laboratory

11 *Current scientific and technical reports* (Monthly), National Aeronautical Laboratory

12 *Current technical information* (Monthly), Hindustan Machine Tools Ltd, Bangalore

13 *Bibliography on numerical control of machine tools* (Monthly), Hindustan Machine Tools, Bangalore

14 *Library bulletin for food science and technology* (Monthly), Central Food Tecnological Research Institute

15 *Documentation list for food technology* (Monthly), Central Food Technological Research Institute

16 *Library bulletin* (Monthly), Central Food Technological and Research Institute

17 *Defood abstracts* (Monthly), Defence Food Research Institute

18 *Fishery and marine sciences abstracts* (Quarterly), Regional Centre of the Central Marine Fisheries Research Institute (I C A R)

19 *Current leather literature* (Monthly), Central Leather Research Institute

20 *Leather title service* (Irregular), Central Leather Research Institute

21 *Indian packaging abstracts* (Monthly), Indian Packaging Institute

22 *Monthly bulletin of Documentation in social work and related fields* (Monthly), Delhi School of Social work.

Some of these documentation lists reach beyond the walls of the specialist library for whose use they are prepared. This fact adds its own value to the furtherance of documentation work.

6 Performance: Documentation Service

The systematic production of the 54 documentation lists may be taken as an index to the serious specialised documentation service being done in our specialist libraries.

7 Sample of Documentation Service

I should like to make a suggestion to our Alumni and to other documentalists. It will be of great mutual help if each year, the documentalist of each specialist library, sends to the Annual Seminar of DRTC a detailed account of the most outstanding Specialised Documentation Service done by him in the year. It should describe the happenings at the various stages from the moment the documentalist and the specialist reader contacted each other, till the reader got the documents to his satisfaction. It should give a detailed account of the trilogue, the various routes — fruitful, semifruitful, and unfruitful — taken in finding the documents for the reader free from "Noise" and "Leakage". The Chapter on "Illustrative Actualities" given in my *Reference service* (1965) may serve as a sample. The reports on the current year's actualities in different libraries will lead to a useful discussion during the Seminar. It will create also a spirit of emulation in all the documentalists. In due course, this feature of the Annual Seminar of DRTC will lead at least to developmental research in improving the techniques of documentation work and service if not to fundamental research.

CHAPTER J

INDIAN NATIONAL SCIENTIFIC DOCUMENTATION CENTRE

1 Genesis

11 Attempt 1 to Establish a National Documentation Centre

Chap f has given an account of the first attempt made in 1947 to establish a National Documentation Centre in India. As stated in that Chap, this attempt proved abortive on account of the current meaning of the terms 'Document' and 'Documentation' not having been understood properly in India and in some other countries at that time. The proposal was merely "filed" by the Education Ministry of the Government of India.

12 Attempt 2 to Establish a National Documentation Centre

In 1950, Sir Santhi Swarup Bhatnagar, the Secretary of the Ministry of Natural Resources and Scientific Research, took over for a few months the additional charge of the Secretaryship of the Ministry of Education. Sir Maurice Gwyer, Vice-Chancellor of the University of Delhi, seems to have told Bhatnagar about my abortive attempt in 1947. Bhatnagar traced out the file from the archives (!) of the Ministry of Education. He told me that there would be no chance for the success of my proposal, if it were left in the hands of the Ministry of Education. He also asked me whether there was any objection to his transferring the file to his own care in the Ministry of Natural Resources and Scientific Research. I welcomed the proposal. This initiated attempt 2.

13 Scheme 1 on the Subject

Bhatnagar asked me to work out a scheme for developing a National Documentation Centre. At that time, there was not much demand for specialised documentation work. The main function of the Centre was decided as doing some documentation work so as to stimulate a demand for it. Further, there was hardly any trained documentalist to man the Centre. Therefore, I thought that it would be too uneconomical to start the Centre in a large way. I decided to

1 Head the National Documentation Centre myself in an honorary capacity;

2 Keep its Office free of rent in my house; and

3 Publish a periodical documentation list, with the help of a small staff, giving them the necessary in-training.

On this basis I worked out a scheme costing only Rs 25,000 per year.

14 Scheme 2 on the Subject

On receiving my Scheme 1, Bhatnagar said that the Government would not consider any Scheme costing less than about Rs 200,000 per year. For this reason, he asked me to put up another scheme with liberal financial provisions, and not a miserly one as my Scheme 1 was. Accordingly, my Scheme 2 was prepared, requiring an annual expenditure of about Rs 200,000.

15 Scheme 3 on the Subject

On receiving my Scheme 2 Bhatnagar was faced with the policy of the Government that any scheme costing Rs 100,000 or more, per year, needed the sanction of the Cabinet, and it may be difficult to secure it as the idea of Documentation was too new for the Cabinet or for the Secretariat concerned to accept it.

Therefore, he asked me to put up another scheme, involving an annual cost slightly less than Rs 100,000. Accordingly, my Scheme 3 was prepared and sent to Bhatnagar. To work out the details he appointed a Committee consisting of himself as Chairman, myself as Member-Secretary, and Sir K S Krishnan as Member. On 25 January 1950, the Committee decided to

1 Enrol India as a National Member of the FID;

2 Establish a National Documentation Centre for India; and

3 Ask me to prepare a note describing the work to be done by the Centre and indicating the initial expenditure required.

My note was approved. Such was the genesis of the Insdoc.

2 Managerial Set-Up

21 Help Sought Under Unesco's Technical Assistance Programme

Bhatnagar wanted to put in more money into the affair, than the one mentioned in my Scheme 3 (*See* Sec H15). Therefore, he suggested that the help of Unesco might be sought. In April 1950, I was invited by Unesco (Paris) to work out a memorandum on "Classification, Coding, and Machinery for Search". Bhatnagar and Krishnan asked me to use that opportunity to negotiate with Unesco for a grant-in-aid to our proposed National Documentation Centre under its Technical Assistance Programme. The Unesco gave its general approval to this request of India.

22 Finalisation of Unesco's Help

The Ministry for Natural Resources and Scientific Research appointed a Committee consisting of Bhatnagar as

Chairman and Krishnan, myself, and a Representative of the Ministry of Education, as members, to finalise the arrangements for the establishment of a National Documentation Centre. The first meeting of the Committee was held on 14 November 1950. Dr Malcolm Adiseshiah of the Unesco attended the Meeting as its Representative. On the strong insistence of the Chairman, the proposal of the Unesco Representative sending a foreigner as the Director of the Centre was disapproved on the ground that India herself had an internationally recognised documentation expert. The main object of the Centre was decided to be doing Documentation work for the benefit of the existing and projected national laboratories, scientific research institutions, technological institutions, universities, branches of industries etc, and in general, to help stimulation of research in India and the avoidance of unintentionally taking up any item of research already completed elsewhere. It was agreed that the Unesco would

1	Award fellowships and study grants for study abroad to the equivalent of	\$ 8,000
2	Supply technical and other equipments to the equivalent of	\$ 24,000
3	Supply scientific periodicals to the equivalent of	\$ 13,000
	Total	\$ 45,000

4 Maintain three foreign experts for three years.

23 Government of India's Approval

In September 1951, the Government of India approved the scheme for the National Documentation Centre and sanctioned the following:

1 An annual expenditure of Rs 94,500 as given in Scheme 3 (*See* Sec H15);

2 The location of the Centre in the National Physical Laboratory, Hill Side Road, New Delhi;

3 The Centre functioning as the clearing house for micro ideas passing into India from outside and from India to outside in all the subjects; and

4 The Centre working under the Director-General of the CSIR (Council of Scientific and Industrial Research).

24 Advisory Committee

In 1951, the Government of India appointed an Advisory Committee to advise the Director-General of the CSIR about the management of the National Documentation Centre. The Director-General was its *ex-officio* Chairman and the Head of the Centre its Secretary. The first meeting of this Committee was held on 8 February 1952. In this meeting it was decided to restrict the sphere of the Centre to Natural Sciences and their applications. Therefore, it was named, "Indian National Scientific Documentation Centre"—shortened form "Insdoc"—, instead of "Indian National Documentation Centre" to cover all subjcts. This meeting also spelt out the objectives of the Insdoc in detail. These were determined to be

1 Receive and retain all scientific periodicals which may be of use to the country;

Note.—This was to be a temporary function till a National Science Library could be established.

2 Issue a monthly "Abstracts of Papers" likely to be of interest to scientists and engineers;

Note.—On grounds of viability and time factor "Abstracts" was changed into "Insdoc list." This was to give only a classified list of the titles of the current papers.

3 Answer specific queries of a documentation nature, from the information accessible to the Insdoc;

4 Supply, on request, reprographs of papers to libraries or to individual specialists at an approved standard rate of price;

5 Supply, on request, translations of papers to libraries or to individual specialists at an approved standard rate of price;

6 Be a national depository for reports of the scientific work of the nation, both published and unpublished; and

Note.—same as under category 1.

7 Be a channel for exchange of information between India and other countries in respect of scientific work in progress.

25 SUB-COMMITTEE OF THE ADVISORY COMMITTEE

The Advisory Committee appointed the following sub-committees with me as Chairman:

1 Technical Sub-Committee, to examine and advise on technical matters connected with documentation work;

2 Classification Sub-Committee, to have charge of details of classification and its continuing improvement;

3 Editorial Sub-Committee, to recommend on the documentation periodicals of the Insdoc—*Insdoc list* and *Bibliography of scientific publications of South and South East Asia*; and

4 Budget Sub-Committee, to prepare the annual budget and present it to the Advisory Committee.

3 Decade 1: Conformity to Approved Policy

31 STAFF

The office of the Insdoc was formed in January 1952. By 1962, excluding those engaged in the library (which was only a temporary charge of Insdoc) the staff of the Insdoc had grown to 96. The following were the Foreign Experts deputed by the Unesco to work in the Insdoc, for a period of three years;

1 Mr J B Reid for Documentation Work in general, joined in January 1952;

2 Mr A L Gardner for Translation, joined in April 1952; and

3 Mr A A Pelletier for Printing and Reprography, joined in November 1952.

32 *Insdoc list*: Form of Presentation of Entries

I was chairman of the Technical Sub-Committee. The Foreign Experts were invited to attend its first meeting, as observers. The Sub-Committee decided that the two documentation periodicals—*Insdoc list* and the *Bibliography of scientific publications of South and South East Asia* should be of the classified variety using the Indian scheme, Colon Classification. But according to the Foreign Expert for Translation the *Insdoc list* should only reproduce the contents page of each of the periodicals covered by it. This suggestion was not accepted by the Sub-Committee. But the Head of the Insdoc wrongly sent the draft minutes of the meeting to the Foreign Experts, before getting the approval of the Chairman. They wrote a dissenting minute against the classified presentation of the entries in the *Insdoc list*. The Chairman pointed out that:

1 The Foreign Experts were only invitees and not members of the Sub-Committee; therefore,

2 They were not entitled to write a dissenting minute.

This matter was raised in the next meeting by the Foreign Experts. According to them,

1 They acted as advisers on behalf of the Unesco; and

2 The advice given by them should be recorded in the minutes.

The Chairman gave the following ruling:

1 The responsibility of the advisers ended with their giving advice to the meeting;

2 It was for the Sub-Committee to accept it or not; and

3 It was not necessary to state in the minutes the advice given by the Foreign Experts.

321 *The Translation Expert Becomes Adviser to Pakistan on Documentation*

In 1956, the Translation Expert got himself nominated as an expert adviser to the Pakistan National Scientific and Technical Documentation Centre! There he succeeded in making their documentation periodical to consist merely of the reproduction of the contents pages of the periodicals covered. This petty detail is mentioned here to show the danger involved in inviting Foreign Experts to advise us on vital matters.

33 *Insdoc list* GETS STARTED

The first issue of the *Insdoc list* came out on 1 June 1954. It was a fortnightly issued on the 1st and 16th of each month. Normally, it covered about 650 periodicals. Each issue gave a classified list of about 2,000 papers.

34 *Bibliography of scientific publications*

The first issue of the *Bibliography of scientific publications of South and South East Asia* came out in April 1955. It was a quarterly from Volume 1 to 3 (1955–57). From

Vol 4 (1958) it was made a monthly. In this documentation list also the entries were arranged in a classified sequence according to the Colon Classification. Normally, it covered about 300 scientific periodicals, published in eight countries of South East Asia. Each issue listed about 550 papers with abstracts. This publication was taken over by the Unesco in 1959.

35 *Union Catalogue*

In 1952, with the aid of the Unesco and on behalf of the Indian Library Association. I had brought out a *Union catalogue of learned periodicals in South East Asia.* This was done in advance as an essential tool for the work of the Insdoc. The cabinet containing the cards forming the originals of the entries in the printed catalogue, was transferred to the Insdoc. According to the then expectation the Insdoc was to keep the Union Catalogue-in-card ever up-to-date. Further, the Insdoc should publish a second edition of the *Union catalogue* in respect of India, after a period of about ten years. The Insdoc appointed a special staff for the latter purpose, and the matter for the second edition was ready by the end of 1962 — when I still continued to be a Member of the Advisory Committee and the Chairman of the Technical Sub-Committee.

36 General Progress

The progress in the work of the Insdoc was steady throughout its first decade, though slow when compared with the progress of the Viniti of U S S R, also established in 1952 (*See* Sec B3). Nor can the organisation of the work in the Insdoc be said to have been as efficient as that of Viniti. But all the intended activities were being carried out. However, the quality of its documentation periodicals was not second to that of any published anywhere else. I am basing this on the testimony of several documentalists met by me in International Conferences.

37 Inadequacy of Public Relation Work

One of the reasons for the Insdoc going slow might have been the absence of adequate public relation work with the specialist libraries and research workers.

38 Proposal for Doubling the Work Load and the Budget

381 *Proposal Approved and Implemented*

Early in 1959, the Director-General of the CSIR appointed me as a One-Man Committee to work out a scheme for the expansion of the work of the Insdoc, during the Third Five Year Plan period beginning with 1961-62. I was also appointed a member of the Working Party of Scientists formed for formulating the Plan for Scientific and Industrial Research. My draft plan was generally approved by the Working Party, and later by the Planning Commission. It was also accepted by the Government of India for implementation.

382 *Basis of the Scheme*

My scheme was a projection of the experience gained by the Insdoc till 1958. It was based on the anticipated increasing tempo of industrialisation and research in the country.

383 *Target of the Scheme*

The target of my scheme was:

1 The coverage of at least 3,000 periodicals of the world, by the *Insdoc list*, requiring about 8,000 entries in each issue;

2 Inclusion of additional subject fields in the coverage of the *Insdoc list*;

3 Exhaustive coverage of all the scientific periodicals published in India;

4 Increase in the Annual Budget from Rs 4 lakhs to Rs 30 lakhs;

Note.—

1 The increased amount covered also the Budget for the National Science Library to be formed, but this does not strictly belong to the Insdoc Budget. So it must be excluded.

2 The increased amount included also the Budget for the Research and Training Department. It was felt that the Insdoc should be saddled with this work till it would be taken over by a University or by any other body organised for this purpose. In view of this, the Director-General of the CSIR had welcomed the formation of the DRTC (= Documentation Research and Training Centre) for this purpose and asked the Insdoc not to take up this activity (*See* Sec F22). So the proposed annual Budget stands considerably reduced, except for the increase due to the increase in the number of periodicals covered, increase in the cost of periodicals and of the equipment, and also increase in staff salary taking place in the country in general.

5 Provision, for capital expenditure as follows:

51 Building for the Insdoc	Rs 10 lakhs
52 Machinery for the physical production of documentation periodicals and lists	Rs 7 lakhs
Total capital expenditure for Insdoc	Rs 17 lakhs

6 Provision for capital expenditure for the science library, as follows:

61 Building	Rs 10 lakhs
62 Back volumes of periodicals	Rs 5 lakhs
Total capital expenditure for the Science Library	Rs 15 lakhs

Note.—This does not however strictly belong to Insdoc.

4 Decade 2: Deviation from the Approved Purpose and Policy

From about 1963, the performance of the Insdoc has undergone much of defraction from the policy laid down by its Authorities at the time of its foundation. There was also a considerable defraction from the purposes approved by the Government, to be served by the increasing budget.

41 'Insdoc list' Abandoned

For one reason or another, the publication of the *Insdoc list,* the primary activity of the Insdoc, was abandoned in 1964, the second year of the second decade. This was in my opinion an unfortunate change. I do not know whether the sanction of the Government of India or of the CSIR, or at least of the Advisory Committee obtained for this abandonment of the primary purpose of the Insdoc.

42 Edition 2 of 'Union Catalogue of Periodicals'

421 *Press Copy for Edition 2 Abandoned*

The copy of the matter for Edition 2 of the *Union catalogue of scientific periodicals* had been prepared and kept ready by the end of 1962. But due to the slowness of work in the Insdoc or to some other reason its printing had not been started immediately. Later the printing of Ed 2 of the *Union Catalogue* was abandoned. Here again, I do not know if the sanction of any higher authority for this change of policy, was taken. Whatever it be, this was the second unfortunate change in policy.

422 *Adoption of an Alternative Costly Method*

On the contrary, the staff of the Insdoc has been sent to each of the libraries in some of the different areas of the country — cities or regions — to catalogue its holdings of periodical publications, *ab initio* and to produce a Local or Regional Union Catalogue. The employment of the Insdoc staff in doing the cataloguing work of the other libraries had never been contemplated. It was improper to make the extra staff sanctioned for other important purposes, do the cataloguing in the different libraries in the country. In one case, even in one and the same locality, a Union Catalogue had been published for a single subject only. But in spite of this, not only the money already spent in the preparation of the press copy for Ed 2 of the Classified Union Catalogue stood totally wasted, but also far more money had been spent in preparing, printing, and publishing different Local Union Catalogues and Local Subject Union Catalogues. Moreover, their usefulness to specialists was far less than that of an All India Union Catalogue. Here again, I do not know whether the sanction of any competent authority for this more costly but less useful operation than the earlier one, was taken.

423 *Single vs Multiple Union Catalogue*

During the long experience, a single omnibus Union Catalogue of the holdings of learned periodicals in all the branches of the Natural Sciences in all the libraries of the country, has been found to be more useful to users, and less costly to prepare, and therefore less costly to purchasers, than a multiple Union Catalogue for each of the different localities and regions in the country and for each of the subjects in the Natural Sciences. The result of this long experience was verified on the basis of an objective case study, by Mr M K Buckland. His findings were published in the *Journal of documentation* (23; 1967; 20–27). The following is a summary of his findings:

"A system of multiple union catalogues differs from a single union catalogue system in the following respects:

"It [the former] is necessarily more expensive to compile and edit. It cannot be less, and is almost certain to be more expensive in terms of catalogue searching. In the case considered it was 1.46 times more expensive. The cost of overheads is likely to be greater. The time taken cannot be less and is almost certain to be greater, being so by a factor of at least 1.23 in the case studied. To perpetuate the existing British multiple union catalogue system or to adopt any system involving more than one union catalogue would be to deliberately incur unnecessary cost, waste scarce skilled labour, and cause unjustifiable delays for readers ... Dr Urquhart and Miss Bunn have demonstrated that at any given level of demand and satisfaction, fewer loanable copies of an item are needed if provision is made on a national rather than a regional basis and that this difference increases sharply as the level of demand rises. This remains just as true whether stock for loan or locations in a union catalogue are considered. It is in precisely the same way that at any given level of demand and satisfaction, a single union catalogue system will require fewer locations than a multiple union catalogue system and that this difference increases sharply as the level of demand rises."

424 *Agency for the care of Union Catalogue*

The National Service Library for Natural Sciences has now been well established. Therefore, the time has come for the responsibility for the publication and maintenance of the Union Catalogue of learned periodicals in the Natural Sciences to be taken away from the Insdoc and handed over to the National Service Library in the Natural Sciences.

43 Classified vs Alphabetical Union Catalogue

The Classified pattern of Ed 1 of the *Union catalogue of learned periodicals* had been found to be helpful not only as a Finding List but also as the basis for important bibliographical research. This has been secured without any appreciable extra cost and without any prejudice whatever, to make the Union Catalogue serve as a Finding List. For, the alphabetical index to the classified part of a Classified Union Catalogue serves as efficiently as an Alphabetical Uunion catalogue as a mere Finding List. This advantage had been fully discussed in a Seminar held in 1959 and published in the *Proceedings* of the Seminar (*See* Sec K3D).

44 Indian Science Abstracts

The publication of the *Indian science abstracts* had been considered and decided against by the Planning Commission on the recommendation of the Working Party of Scientists in 1959. But in 1965, this periodical publication was started by the Insdoc. Whether the sanction for this direct negation of the decision of the Planning Commission was obtained from any competent authority, I do not know.

45 Indian Education Abstracts

In 1969, the Insdoc started the periodical publication *Indian education abstracts*. Its subject "Education" does not belong to the Natural Sciences. It had been decided from the very beginning that the Insdoc should confine its documentation work to Natural Sciences (*See* Sec H2). In fact, its very name — Indian National Scientific Documentation Centre — emphasises this. Further, a periodical giving abstracts of educational papers was already being published by the Ministry of Education of the Government of India. What was the necessity for Insdoc duplicating the work already being done by the Government?

46 Training of Documentalists

The Insdoc runs a School for Training in Documentation since 1964.

47 Formation of a Regional Centre

In 1964, a Regional Centre of the Insdoc was formed in Bangalore, probably because the Parent Body could not cope with the volume of the work. Or was it because the bibliographical requests from South India could be given from Bangalore in an appreciably shorter time than that given from Delhi? If so, what is the average gain in time? What is the extra cost — Recurring cost and Capital cost for building and equipment — involved in opening the Bangalore Branch? In these respects how does the actuality differ from the anticipation? The present day trend — even in countries with a long library and documentation tradition — is to replace an omnibus national library and national documentation centre covering all subjects by different national organisations for different subject fields. Having a single national centre for all subjects and having branches in different parts of the country has been realised to be wasteful and unnecessary. In this connection the change that had occurred in the country in regard to the facilities for inter-library loan and supply of reprograph, should also be taken into consideration.

5 New Venture

According to an agreement signed on 27 February 1970

by the Indo-Soviet Joint Committee for Scientific Collaboration, a project for organising a Russian Science Information Centre was initiated by Insdoc. The objective of the Centre is to acquire current published documents in the field of science and technology brought out in the USSR and to make this available to the scientists, specialists, and institutions of higher education and research in India. Under this agreement, about 3,000 books were received during November 1970 to August 1971 from Viniti. Arrangements have been made to receive 304 current titles of Soviet scientific periodicals. The Russian Science Information Centre would build up a representative collection of reference material on science and technology subjects published in the USSR, a collection of standard monographs and treatises in the fields of natural and applied sciences, science of science, industrial economics, construction engineering, agriculture, informatics, higher education, training of scientific personnel and popular science. The Centre is presently bringing out two lists — "Russian Scientific and Technical Publications — an Accession List" and "Contents List of Society Scientific Periodicals." Both the lists are being distributed free of cost to about 900 scientific institutions.

6 Decade 3: Hope for the Future

Decade 3 of the working of the Insdoc will start shortly. I should like to conclude this Chapter by expressing a wish and a hope:

1 The Insdoc will be put on right rails from decade 3 onwards;

2 It will get decentralised by subjects and/or by catering to the documentation needs of special kinds of research activities;

3 It will not continue as an omnibus documentation centre with omnibus regional branches. However,

4 The cost of printing the documentation periodicals and lists of the different subject-centres for documentation will be minimised by avoiding each documentation centre having its own printing and associated equipment. On the contrary,

5 One and the same plant for printing will be used by the documentation centres for all the subjects.

CHAPTER K

INDIAN NATIONAL SOCIAL SCIENCE DOCUMENTATION CENTRE

1 Genesis of Indian National Social Science Documentation

11 Attempt 1: 1959, Delhi

The Library Seminar on Research in the Social Sciences, held from 2 to 4 January 1959, in Delhi with Sri Girja Kumar as Secretary and myself as Chairman, under the joint auspices of the Indian School of International Studies and the Indian Council of World Affairs, recommended the following:

1 An Indian National Social Science Documentation Centre (Insodoc) should be established; and

2 Its functions should be similar to those of the Insdoc.

The follow-up work on these recommendations was not successful.

12 Attempt 2: 1960, Bangalore

The Seminar on International Relations and Regional Studies held in May-June 1962 in Bangalore with Dr Appadorai as Chairman under the auspices of the School of International Studies, largely composed of university teachers. It recommended the following:

1 A Central Library on International Relations should be established;

2 The activities of the Central Library should be linked up with the work of the proposed Insodoc; and

3 This Centre should be developed on the lines recommended by the Library Seminar on Research in the Social Sciences (1959).

No result came out of this.

13 ATTEMPT 3: 1962, CALCUTTA

A Seminar on Bibliographical Control was held on 10 February 1962 in Calcutta, with B S Kesavan as Director, under the auspices of the Indian Library Association. This was sponsored by the Ministry of Education of the Government of India. According to its recommendations:

1 Documentation work and service should be done in the different subject areas in the social sciences by thirteen different agencies;

2 There should be a coordinating body for all documentation activities in the natural sciences, humanities, and social sciences;

3 A permanent Advisory Committee on Policy should be set up to implement the proposals; and

4 The functions of the coordinating body should be similar to those of the Insdoc, but without those of compiling and publishing an advance documentation list and of abstracts.

No result came out of this attempt.

14 ATTEMPT 4: 1964, LUCKNOW

In its Session on Indian Social Science Documentation, the Iaslic Seminar held from 2 to 6 October 1964, in Lucknow, with N K Goil as Rapporteur and Girja Kumar as Chairman, recommended the following:

1 The functions of the Insodoc should be similar to those of the Insdoc.

2 The Iaslic should request the Central Government to provide funds for the establishment of the Centre and for making a survey of the existing documentation services in Social Sciences in India; and

3 The University Grants Commission should be requested to provide funds for compiling a Union Catalogue of Periodical Publications in Social Sciences.

No result came out of this.

15 ATTEMPT 5: 1965, TRIVANDRUM

In its Session on Social Science Documentation, the Iaslic Conference held on 28 December 1965 in Trivandrum with K S Deshpande as Rapporteur and K S Hingwe as Director, recommended:

1 The question of the centralisation and the decentralisation of documentation services; and

2 A survey of the resources and documentation activities in the social sciences in India.

The result of the survey was to be reported to the Planning Commission by the end of March 1966.

16 ATTEMPT 6: 1967, DELHI

Early in 1967, a survey of the activities in Social Science Documentation in India was made by Girja Kumar on behalf of the Indian Council of World Affairs. The data of this survey formed part of a working paper for the Seminar on Documentation in the Social Sciences held on 25 to 27 February 1967, in Delhi, with Girja Kumar as Secretary and myself as Chairman, under the auspices of the School of International Studies. In the Seminar:

1 The members of the Seminar were divided into a number of groups each with a Chairman and a Rapporteur of its own;

2 In the second Plenary Session held in the forenoon of each day, the issues for consideration were framed;

3 In the afternoon of each day, each of the groups discussed the issues and sent up its recommendation for

consideration in the first Plenary Session in the forenoon of the next day;

4 The recommendations of each of the issues were finalised in the last Plenary Session;

5 These were sent to the Planning Commission, asking for provision of funds.

But, the attempt did not bear fruit.

17 ATTEMPT 7: 1969, DELHI

The facilities for research in Social Sciences had not received much attention for a long time, when compared with the Natural Sciences, taken on hand about 25 years earlier. There are abundant reasons for this delay. But we are not interested in examining them here. On 12 December 1968, by its Resolution No F.9-50/68 Plg, the Central Ministry of Education established the Indian Council of Social Science Research (ICSSR). On 1 October 1969, in its turn, the ICSSR established its Documentation Branch. N M Ketkar, Librarian, Central Secretariat Library, took charge of this Branch on a part-time basis. By the end of 1969, two Documentation Officers and four senior documentation assistants formed the staff. In the first instance Girja Kumar was requested to make a survey of the existing bibliographical services in the field of social sciences and to report the result by September 1970.

2 Difficulty in Social Science Documentation

2a DIFFICULTY ABOUT THE TERMINOLOGY IN DOCUMENTATION

The Social Science documentalists do not appear to have yet familiarised themselves with the elemental technical terms current in the field of documentation. For instance, they do not seem to have distinguished the difference between the terms 'Documentation work' and 'Documentation service'. Or it may be that the documentalists knew this distinction but could not influence their parent body to understand this distinction and use the current technical term in its Annual reports. This is evidenced by the following passage in the *Annual report* 2, 1970-71 (Please note the italicized words in them):

"The Council proposes to set up a National Bibliographical and Documentation *Service*. Under this programme, institutions will be selected in different parts of the country to do bibliographical and documentation *Work* in specified fields for which they have special competence and facilities. For instance, the Indian Society of Agricultural Economics will be requested to do the bibliographical and Documentation *Work* in the field of agricultural economics. The Anthropological Survey of India will do a similar *Service* in the field of anthropology."

2b Difficulty about the Terminology in Social Sciences

In the Natural Sciences, International Committees on Standard Terminology have been functioning for nearly a century. Practically, each subject in that group has a fairly stabilised Technical Terminology. Therefore, a documentalist may not feel much difficulty in understanding the true import of any document to be included in a documentation list or to be brought into use in documentation service. On the contrary, many of the subjects in the Social Sciences present difficulties arising out of unstabilised terminology. Except perhaps in the Main Subject "Law", this factor makes the work of a documentalist in Social Sciences difficult. The whole document may have to be read, perhaps more than once, to fix its Class Number and to write its Abstract. But, now that documentation enters into the field of Social Sciences, there is perhaps a chance for an agreed Standard Terminology in the Social Sciences to be taken up and pursued with vigour.

2c Difficulty in Respect of the Main Subjects Forming the Social Sciences

"Sociology" is unquestionably accepted as a Main Subject in the field of Social Sciences. So also is "Social Work". But, every subject — the entire Universe of Subjects — has a sociological aspect. This tempts the bringing in of any subject into the field of Social Sciences, many subjects from outside its field. An outstanding example is the "Science of Linguistics". Normally, it is taken to fall within the group of Humanities. But, since language is the medium of communication in any social group, some social scientists would include it among Social Sciences. On the other hand, the Main Subject "Law" can arise only in relation to man in society. Therefore, it should be taken unquestionably as a Social Science. However, on account of the extreme specialisation of this subject, some social scientists would admit only the sociological aspects of "Law" as falling within Social Sciences. The Main Subject "Psychology" is another problem. We should strictly distinguish between the psychology of an individual living within his normal social group or within an alien social group on the one side, and the psychology of a social group — as distinguished from that of an individual — on the other side. The latter certainly falls within Sociology, a Main Subject in Social Sciences. But the former cannot be said to do so, with equal certitude. Many take Psychology to be a Main Subject in the Humanities. However, the psychology of a social group is taken as a compound subject going with the Main Subject "Sociology"

2d Suggested Schedule of Main Subjects in Social Sciences

Perhaps, the table given below may be taken to enumerate the different Main Subjects in Social Sciences as judged by having literary warrant today.

SN	CCN	Main Subject	SN	CCN	Main Subject
1	2	Library science	16	VX	Technique of historical Source
2	2V	Library service (Library science-in-action)	17	W	Political science
3	2YT	Librametry	18	WX	Geopolitics
4	8	Management science	19	X	Economics-in-theory
5	9b	Career	20	XV	Economics-in-action in a territory
6	9p	Conference methodology	21	XX	Economics-in-theory of business enterprise
7	9r	Seminar methodology			
8	9t	Commission methodology	22	XY1	International economics
			23	XYT	Econometrics
9	9P	Communication theory	24	XYV	Economico-cybernetics
10	9Q	Symbolism	25	Y	Sociology
11	T	Education	26	YX	Social work
12	TYT	Educametry	27	YYT	Sociometry
13	TYV	Educational cybernetics	28	YYV	Socio-cybernetics
14	U	Geography	29	Z	Law
15	V	History	30	ZX	Jurisprudence

2e Traditional Main Subjects

The following eight Main Subjects in the field of Social Sciences had acquired literary warrant sufficiently early. Therefore they have been generally included among traditional Main Subjects:

SN	Subject	SN	Subject
1	Library service (Library economy)	5	Political science
2	Education	6	Economics
3	Geography	7	Sociology
4	History	8	Law

2f Scattered Main Subjects

The above table shows that in C C, "Library work or Library economy" stands scattered outside the compact range of Social Science Main Subjects. The following ten Main Subjects also stand scattered outside the compact range of Social Science Main Subjects:

SN	Subject	SN	Snbject
1	Library Science	5	Seminar methodology
2	Management Science	6	Commission methodology
3	Career	7	Communication theory
4	Conference methodology	8	Symbolism

2g Distilled Main Subjects

The eight Main Subjects mentioned in Sec 2f are not Traditional Main Subjects. These Subjects have begun to attract literary warrant only during recent years. All of these will require their respective schedule of isolates. For "Library science" and for "Management science" such schedules have been already enumerated in C C to meet the actual requirements. The other six Main Subjects will have to be taken up at no distant date. Before their gaining the status of a Main Subject, the ideas denoted by them have been occurring only as facets of compound subjects going with some if not all the Traditional Main Subjects. For example, "Management" has been occurring as a facet in Compound Subjects going with subjects such as Economics, Education, Home science, Hospital, Laboratory, and Observatory. In all these subjects we come across "Management-in-action". But a comparative study of Management-in-action in several contexts has now led to the formation of "Management-in-theory." This may be taken to have been "distilled out" of "Management-in-action". Therefore, they are called Distilled Main Subjects.

As the Distilled Main Subjects have affiliation with many of the Main Subjects in a general schedule, it was felt desirable to take them out of the compact range of the Schedule of Traditional Main Subjects of Social sciences. Therefore, they are put prior to the Traditional Main Subjects of all kinds.

Another Distilled Main Subject, "Techniques of Historical Sources" has, however, been given a place in C C within the compact range of the Traditional Main Subjects of Social Sciences.

2h Adjunct and Fused Main Subjects

The following table gives the thirteen Adjunct Main Subjects belonging to the field of Social Sciences:

SN	Fused Main Subject	SN	Fused Main Subject
1	Librametry	7	International economics
2	Educametry	8	Econometrics
3	Educational cybernetics	9	Economico-cybernetics
4	Geopolitics	10	Social work
5	Economics-in-action	11	Sociometry
6	Economics-in-theory of business enterprise	12	Socio-cybernetics
		13	Jurisprudence

2j Difficulty About the Term 'Learned Paper' in Natural Sciences

The term 'Learned Paper' cannot be defined rigorously. However, in the field of Natural Sciences, it is possible to sense the exposition of one and the same subject to be in one or other of the four Standards. A paper of Standard 1 gives the results of research in technical terms. Its readers usually consist of other research workers. A paper of Standard 2 is usually a reproduction of the paper of Standard 1 in a less rigorous style. It is indeed a rehash of the paper of Standard 1, for the use of scholars of Remove one from research workers. A paper of Standard 3 is of a less severe standard than that of Standard 2. This Standard is intended for readers of Remove two — common readers — from research workers. A paper of Standard 4 is an elementary account of anything of Standard 3, suited to students. The following terms used in Sanskrit to denote the four standards are significant:

Standard	Sanskrit term	English translation of the Sanskrit term
1	Prabhu-sammita	Exposition by masters
2	Suhrit-sammita	Exposition by and to friends
3	Kāntā-sammita	Lovers' exposition — that is, intimate exposition in homely language
4	Sisu-sammita	Exposition by and to children

2k Difficulty in the Definition of the Term 'Learned Periodical' in the Natural Sciences

There is difficulty in defining the term 'Learned Periodical'. The following convention was adopted by me while compiling the *Union catalogue of learned periodical publications in South Asia,* Volume 1: *Physical and Biological sciences.* A periodical was deemed to be a learned periodical, if one or other of the following conditions is fulfilled:

1 Majority of the papers in it are learned papers; or

2 At least one paper in each volume is a learned paper; or

3 At least one paper in a few of the volumes is a learned paper.

2m Inclusion of the Periodicals in a Union Catalogue

In a Union Catalogue of Periodicals in Natural Sciences, it is relatively easy to confine the selection of the periodicals to learned periodicals only.

2n Difficulty of the Recognition of a Learned Paper in Social Sciences

In the field of Social Sciences, the exposition of one and the same idea in four different standards, beginning with Standard 1 and ending with Standard 4, is not often found. Therefore, consistent judgement is not easy to be exercised in identifying a learned paper in Social Sciences.

2p Difficulty in Selecting a Learned Periodical in Social Sciences

A consequence of the difficulty in recognising a learned paper in Social Sciences leads naturally to the difficulty in deciding the learned periodicals for inclusion in the Union Catalogue of Periodicals in Social Sciences. The temptation will generally be to include, in the Union Catalogue, Periodicals of Standard 2 also. But this difficulty cannot be altogether overcome because of the very slight distinction between papers of Standard 1 and Standard 2. But papers of Standard 3 and 4 should certainly be omitted in the Union Catalogue.

2q Papers in Newspapers and Newspaper-like Publications

A newspaper — daily or weekly — seldom has a learned paper in Natural Sciences. If at all, papers of Standard 3 may occasionally occur and of Standard 2 even more rarely. Therefore, newspapers and newspaper-like publications can be omitted altogether in a Union Catalogue of Periodicals in Natural Sciences. But in the field of social sciences, a newspaper often contains a paper of Standard 2 and even of Standard 1. The Social Sciences deal with social groups — international, national, etc — practically all possible social groups enumerated in the schedule of isolates of social groups needed in the classification of compound subjects in "Sociology". And human qualities change as often and very often as violently as weather does. Therefore, records of all such social phenomena form necessarily the basis of research in Social Sciences. And newspapers very often form the only source for accounts of such social phenomena. Therefore, while it is not practicable to include all newspapers and newspaper-like publications in the Union Catalogue, there should be a method of bringing the important papers in them to the notice of the research workers in Social Sciences.

2r A Method for Dealing With Newspaper Articles

I was struck by a remarkable method in which newspaper articles of value in Social Sciences were being brought to the notice of research workers by the Institute for International Affairs at the Chatham House, London. I saw a band of documentalists scanning through several newspapers, making a cutting of each article of research value, mounting it on a cardboard of uniform size, and filing all such cuttings in a helpful sequence. This battery of cuttings was being used by several workers. Its service is made to reach throughout the world by the annual digest of such cuttings published as *Survey of international affairs*, the well known product of the editorial skill of Toynbee.

Another publication providing a similar service at present is the *Keesings contemporary archives* (1931—). It is a weekly diary of important events in all countries, abstracted from news agencies' reports, official sources and the principal newspapers of each country.

2s Partial Application of the Method in India

At the request of the Secretary of the All India Congress Committee, it was possible for me to give a memorandum on a similar work to be done in India (See my *Library Tour 1948, Europe and America. Impressions and*

Reflections, 1950, pp. 74–78). Girja Kumar has been doing a similar work in his Library at New Delhi. But I do not know whether a digest from these cuttings, made from any angle, is being published as a substitute for a Union Catalogue of Newspapers.

2t GOVERNMENTAL AND OTHER SERIALS

An authentic source for research in Social Sciences is found in serials — Governmental or Institutional — such as administration reports, and statistical tables. These should certainly be included in a Union Catalogue of Periodical Publications (that is, periodical and serial) in Social Sciences.

3 Right Functions of the Insodoc

The following are the right functions of the Insodoc:

1 Publishing a periodical advance documentation list of the papers appearing in the current issues of the periodicals in Social Sciences taken in India;

2 Supplying or arranging for the supply of the translation of any paper to any service library or even to any individual reader, and for this purpose maintaining a panel of translators of papers in every possible combination of "Language and Subject" likely to be needed in the country;

3 Supplying or arranging for the supply of reprograph of any paper to any service library or even to any individual reader, and for this purpose maintaining a reprographing unit;

4 Publishing a biennial list of Social Science periodicals currently taken in the libraries in India;

5 Publishing at suitable intervals, the Union Catalogue of Social Science Periodical Publications in the libraries in India;

6 Arranging for inter-library loan, in order to maximise the use of the periodical publications available in the different libraries; and

7 Preparing a documentation list of the doctoral theses approved by the Indian Universities.

3a Periodical Publication of a Documentation List

The Periodical Publication of an advance documentation list is the primary function of the Insodoc. This has been altogether lost sight of and not mentioned in any of the documents published by the ICSSR as the function of the Insodoc. Whether the abandoning of this primary function by the Insdoc during its decade 2 had been responsible for this serious omission is not known. (*See* Sec J41). This primary function will have to be carried out as mentioned below. The Insodoc,

1 Should acquire by air mail, a microfilm copy of the contents page of the issue, being currently produced, of each of the learned periodicals taken in the country in its subject field; or if it is too costly,

2 Acquire by air mail, a proof copy of each of the contents pages;

3 Make a classified catalogue of the papers in the contents pages, with a direct or indirect bearing on the research work in progress in the country, with all the limitations imposed on classification by the absence of the full text of the papers;

4 Print periodically — say, once in a fortnight or once in a month — and send out copies of the classified catalogue, mentioned in category 3, to each of the participating specialists and other libraries in the country; so that

5 The classified catalogue reaches each participating library before or on the same day as the full issues covered by it reach it.

A twofold purpose will be served by such an advance documentation periodical. It will appetize the research workers and make them ask for and read the papers in the list relevant to their field of work. It will also help the avoidance of unintentionally duplicating any investigation already in progress or completed anywhere in the world.

3b Translation Service

For the time being English may be taken to be the language in use among the Social Scientists in India. Therefore, translations of papers from any other language may have to be provided now and again. The Insodoc should arrange for such translation service. In this connection it must be remembered that every person capable of translating an ordinary passage may not be able to translate a scientific passage correctly. For this purpose we want a person with a double qualification — "Language *cum* Subject Qualification". In India, the demand for translation from any language is not likely to justify, for many years, the employment of a team of translators on a full-time salary basis. The economical way will be to get the translation done on piece-work basis by a panel of private translators. The Insodoc should carefully select one or two persons with each such "Language *cum* Subject Qualification." A panel of such persons for all combinations of subjects and languages should be maintained by Insodoc and brought up to date from time to time. The panel should include specialist translators living not only in Delhi, but also in other cities of the country, wherever it is possible. A copy of the panel giving details about the name, the address, and the Language *cum* Subject Qualification should be supplied to each of the participating service libraries. Secondly, each of the participating service libraries is expected to have with it a copy of the Biennial List of the Social Science periodicals currently taken in India and of the Union Catalogue.

When a reader asks his local service library for the translation of a paper, its librarian should find out whether a copy of the translation of the paper is in the Translation Pool of the Insodoc. If it is, he must procure a copy of the translation from the Insodoc. If it is not in the Translation Pool he should find out from the Biennial List or from the Union Catalogue the nearest library having a copy of the paper. He should also find out from the Panel of Translators the name and address of the possible translator of the paper. If these two are within his easy reach, he may himself arrange for the translation. He should make two copies of the translation — one for the reader concerned and the other for the "Translation Pool" maintained by the Insodoc. If the conditions are not favourable for the librarian of the local service library for himself to arrange for the translation, he may pass on the request to the Insodoc for compliance. There is nothing gained by mechanically passing on to the Insodoc every request for translation. This will only increase the load on the Insodoc and cause time lag in the supply of the translation. A convenient staggering of the translation work among the Insodoc and the participating local service libraries will add to efficiency and promptness of supply. On the other hand centralisation will deny these benefits, and will bring disrepute to the service.

3c Reprography Service

When a reader asks his local service library for a reprograph of a paper, its librarian should find out whether the original of the paper is available in his own library, or in any other library of his own locality, or find out the nearest library having the original. He should also find out if there is a reprograph equipment available in any of the libraries located by him. If not he should find out if a commercial reprographing agency exists in any of the localities concerned. If these conditions are satisfied the librarian of the local service library may himself arrange for the supply of the reprograph. If the conditions are not favourable for the librarian of the local service library for himself to arrange for the reprograph, he may pass on the request to the Insodoc for compliance. There is nothing gained by mechanically passing on to the Insodoc every request for reprograph, particularly because, during the last ten years many places have commercial reprographing agencies; and the liberal book-grant received from the University Grants Commission enables many libraries to subscribe for a fairly large number of periodicals in the Social Sciences. Otherwise it will only increase the load on the Insodoc and cause time lag in the supply of the reprograph. A convenient staggering of the reprographing work among the Insodoc and the participating local service libraries will add to efficiency and promptness of supply. On the other hand centralisation will deny these benefits, and the time lag will bring disrepute to the service.

3d Biennial List of Learned Periodicals and Serials Currently Taken in India

The Biennial List of the Social Science periodicals and serials currently being taken in India is necessary to keep up to date the Union Catalogue of periodicals maintained by the Insodoc. The first Biennial List may, if preferred, be prepared simultaneously with the first edition of the Union Catalogue. This would result in great economy, though it may mean a delay of perhaps two years. It has to be considered whether the avoidance of the delay of two years would be sufficient compensation for the extra-money to be spent on producing the Biennial List immediately.

3e/3W Union Catalogue of Learned Periodicals and Serials in India

3e *Learned Periodical*

The various difficulties met with by me in the definition of a Learned Periodical while preparing the *Union Catalogue* in 1953, and the extent to which they could be minimised have been briefly described in Sec 2j to 2p and have been fully described in Chap RA of my *Classified catalogue code*, Ed 5, 1964 (*CCC*).

3f/38 Procedure

3f *Libraries with Very Large Concentration of Learned Periodicals and Serials*

There are said to be about 4,000 learned periodicals and serials in Social Sciences in the libraries of Delhi taken together. One or other of each is said to be available in one or more libraries in Delhi. It is doubtful, if there will be even as many as 500 to 1,000 additional learned periodicals and serials in any other locality in India. Most of these additional learned periodicals are likely to be found in about ten large university libraries.

3g *Procedure to Collect Information*

To collect the information at the cheapest and the most accurate and expeditious way the procedure described in the succeeding sections is suggested. It is now being formulated on the basis of the experience gained by me in compiling and publishing the *Union Catalogue of learned periodical publications in South Asia*, Volume 1: *Physical and biological sciences* (1953). The procedure suggested now eliminates some of the difficulties met with in the above mentioned first attempt made about 20 years ago.

3h *Stages*

The procedure should be divided into the following nine stages:

1 Making the Union Catalogue for the libraries of Delhi;

2 Sending two copies of the Delhi Union Catalogue to the libraries outside Delhi, expected to have a fairly good collection of learned periodicals and serials in the Social Sciences, along with a letter describing the work to be done by each participating library;

3 Consolidating the entries relating to Delhi and to the other areas mentioned in Stage 2;

4 During the process of consolidation, finding out the name of each of the libraries outside Delhi the information furnished by which is incomplete and needs revision;

5 The Senior Cataloguer visiting those libraries and completing their respective returns, and also visiting any other libraries conjectured or known to have some learned periodical or serial, not found in the libraries already covered, and making the entries for them;

6 Merging the fresh entries got in Stage 5, into the consolidated Union Catalogue in cards and slips respectively;

7 Preparing the press copy of the Union Catalogue with the help of the slips;

8 Printing and publishing the Union Catalogue;

9 Preserving the Union Catalogue in cards for future use when a revised edition becomes necessary.

Each stage of procedure may involve different steps of work.

3j/3v The Steps in Stage 1: Completion of the Delhi Union Catalogue

3j *Step* 1 *in Stage* 2: *Technical Personnel Needed*

At least two persons with full competence in cataloguing learned periodicals and serials will be required in Step 1 of Stage 1. Each should be thoroughly familiar with the application of the Rules for meeting all the 19 idiosyncrasies of learned periodicals enumerated in Chap PA of *CCC*. Each should also be familiar with the Rules for cataloguing learned periodicals and serials, given in Chap PB to PJ of *CCC*. Each should also be familiar with the Rules on Union Catalogue given in Chap RB to RP of *CCC*. Let us call the two persons A and B. For convenience let us assume that A is abler than B.

3k *Step 2 in Stage* 1: *Selection and Training of the Personnel*

The work attempted is a very important one; it is also a costly one; it may not be easy to re-do it for another two decades at least. Therefore, the work in this first edition of the Union Catalogue of Learned Periodicals and Serials in Social Sciences should be made in the best possible style. Implications: A and B should have the best possible training in this work. Perhaps it will be helpful to send the selected persons — A and B — to a training centre such as the DRTC for two or three months.

3m *Step* 3 *in Stage* 1: *Sequence of Delhi Libraries for Collecting Data*

For organising the initial work to be done by A and B in Delhi, the libraries in Delhi should be arranged in the decreasing sequences of the number of learned periodicals and serials in their respective holdings. Their work in the libraries should begin with the first in the sequence, then pass on to the second in the sequence, and so on.

3n *Step* 4 *in Stage* 1: *Work in Library* 1 *in Delhi*

A and B may start working together in Library 1. This will enable them to get attuned to secure uniformity in preparing the catalogue entries. At a proper stage A and B may be sent to different libraries in order to gain time.

3p *Step* 5 *in Stage* 1: *Preparation of the Basic Catalogue Cards*

The catalogue entries should be entered in 125×75mm catalogue cards. In most cases the main entry of a learned periodical, and occasionally of a serial also, may have to be in several "Continued cards" (*See* Chap EF of *CCC*). There should be a separate continued card for each idiosyncrasy of a learned periodical. The last continued card (or sets of continued cards) should be devoted to the entry of the holdings in the library. There should be also added entries as prescribed. (*See* Sec PB2 to PB5 of *CCC*). Some added entries will occur in the classified part and some in the alphabetical part. We may denote these cards by the term 'Basic Catalogue Cards'. It may be repeated that each of the Basic Catalogue Cards should be in Library Hand and should conform strictly to the Rules of

CCC to every detail — such as, use of capital and lower-case, section formations, and punctuation marks (*See* Chap ED of *CCC*).

3q *Step* 6 *in Stage* 1: *Typing out, on Slips, of Copies of the Basic Catalogue Cards*

At the end of each day the Basic Catalogue Cards prepared during the day should be passed on to the Office of the Insodoc. Three copies of each of the cards should be typed out on 125×75mm slips of thick paper. As soon as work in Library 1 is completed, the typed slips should be sorted out into three sets — to be named A, B, and C. Then the slips in each set should be arranged according to the Rules in Chap EG for the Classified part, and in Chap EH for the Alphabetical part, of *CCC*. Similar work should be done with the Basic Catalogue Cards also.

3r/3v Library 2 onwards in Delhi and Design of Holdings Card

3r *Step* 7 *in Stage* 1: *Work in Library* 2 *Onwards in Delhi*

After the work in Library 1 is finished A and B can be sent to different libraries. When the cataloguers A and B are sent out, A will carry with him the set A of the catalogue slips for work in Library 2. Similarly B will carry with him the set B of the catalogue slips for work in Library 3; and so on. Hereafter the work of A alone will be described and the work of B will be similar. Therefore the term 'cataloguer' will be used instead of A and B. With the help of the catalogue slips the cataloguer will pick out any new learned periodical or serial found in the library. He will then write the Basic Catalogue Cards for each of the new items as described in Sec 3p. He will also find out the learned periodicals and serials already represented in the catalogue slips taken with him. For each of them, he will fill up the Holdings Section for the library in which he works.

3s *Step 8 in Stage 1: New Problems for Decision Making*

Each cataloguer will maintain a diary showing the dates in which work was done in the respective libraries. In the page allotted to a library he will also note any new or difficult problem met with. Before leaving the Insodoc Office each day, A and B should discuss these problems with others and decide the way of dealing with them. Each decision should be entered both in the page allotted to the library and also in the pages allotted for "Decisions", with a cross reference to the page for the library where the problem arose.

3t *Step 9 in Stage 1: Merging of the Basic Catalogue Cards*

At the end of each day, A and B will hand over the Basic Catalogue Cards written on that day to the Office of the Insodoc. The Insodoc Office will type out three sets of copies of the Basic Catalogue Cards as prescribed in Sec 3q. As soon as the work in any library is completed by a cataloguer, the procedure mentioned in Sec 35k should be followed. The new sets of Basic Catalogue Cards pertaining to the library just completed should be merged with the already existing Basic Catalogue Cards cumulating from Step 6 onwards in Stage 1. So also with each set of the typed slips — A, B, and C.

3u *Step 10 in Stage 1: Completion of the Union Catalogue for Delhi*

The cards thus cumulated after the work in the last library in Delhi has been completed will form the Union Catalogue for Delhi. The cards should be securely filed in a cabinet. Similarly, each set of slips also should be filed in a cabinet of its own.

3v *Design of the Holdings Card*

The Holdings Card or a set of them, as the case may be, for each learned periodical and serial should mention the Code Number for each library with sufficient space against each one of them to indicate its holdings of the learned periodical or serial concerned. For example see the sample page given in Annexure 1. For an illustrative full list of Code Numbers for libraries see Sec 3J. In the Union Catalogue the Holdings Card for any specific learned periodical or serial should mention only the Code Numbers of the libraries having it.

3w/3x Production of Copies of the Delhi Union Catalogue and Soliciting Cooperation from each Participating Library of Order 1 Outside Delhi

3w *Step* 1 *in Stage* 2: *Production of Copies of the Delhi Union Catalogue*

With the help of the Slips in Set A, produce a volume of the Delhi Union Catalogue by printing or near-printing process. While printing, between two consecutive main entries a double space, for entering the holdings of the Library in respect of each main entry, should be left. The number of copies to be printed should be determined on the basis of the maximum number of libraries outside Delhi, considered to have an appreciable collection of learned periodicals and serials in Social Sciences. Each copy should be bound interleaved.

I used the slips themselves — numerically numbered — as press copy. This technique is not a common one. But the Times of India Press (Delhi) gave every cooperation in the matter. After a forme of 16 pages was finalised, the press had no difficulty in using the slips as press copy. If this is not practicable the press copy will have to be continuously typed on sheets of paper. Of course, this will add appreciably to the cost of production.

3x *Step 2 in Stage 2: Soliciting Cooperation from each Participating Library of Order 1 Outside Delhi*

To each library of order 1 outside Delhi, selected for inclusion in the Union Catalogue on account of their having an appreciable collection of learned periodicals and serials in Social Sciences, two interleaved copies of the Delhi Union Catalogue should be sent. Each copy should have the Code Number for the library written near the top of the cover, title page, the first page of the text and in a few other standard pages, such as page 50, page 100 etc. and also in the last page of the text. These should be sent along with a covering letter. As it is well known, the good will and cooperation of the librarian may be got by typing out a separate letter to each librarian, instead of using carbon copies or copies got by printing or near-printing processes.

3y/3z Scrutiny of the Entries Furnished by the Libraries of Order 1 Outside Delhi and Supplement 1 to the Delhi Union Catalogue

3y *Step 1 in Stage 3: Scrutiny and Correction, if any, of the New Entries furnished by each Library Outside Delhi*

On the receipt of the fair copy of the Delhi Union Catalogue from each participating Library of order 1 outside Delhi, the Class Numbers and the other details in the new entries made by them in the interleaved copies should be checked and, if necessary, brought into conformity to those used in the Delhi Union Catalogue.

3z *Step 2 in Stage 3: Supplement to the Delhi Union Catalogue*

Consolidate all the new entries into a single supplementary volume, and get interleaved copies of them as prescribed in Sec 3x.

31 *Step 3 in Stage 3: Order 2 Libraries Outside Delhi*

By this time, information would have been received about some other libraries worth being brought into the Union Catalogue, because of their being likely to have a good collection of learned periodicals and serials in Social Sciences. Information of this kind, about such libraries, can be solicited from the librarian of each of the participating libraries of order 1. He is likely to have local knowledge about libraries of order 2 lying within his area.

32 *Steps 4 to 6 in Stage 3: Soliciting Cooperation from the Order 2 Libraries etc*

The procedure in these steps is similar to that described in Sec 3x to 3z.

33 *Stage 4: Detection of Incomplete Information given by any Library Outside Delhi*

During the process of consolidation in Stage 3, incomplete information or information of doubtful reliability, found in the entries of any library, should be detected. All such information should be entered in a helpful way in the diary mentioned in Sec 3s.

34 *Stage 5: Correction and Completion of Errors and Omissions*

The Cataloguer A should visit each of the libraries mentioned in Sec 33 and get the incomplete information completed and bring information of doubtful reliability to full reliability. In this trip, if he hears about any library of order 3 fit to be included in the Union Catalogue, he should collect the necessary information from it.

In my work on the *Union Catalogue* (of 1933), about ten places had to be visited for such work. Nine of them were in India, and the tenth was in Colombo. For getting easy cooperation from the libraries concerned and for expediting the work I myself did this work. Making allowance for the holidays and the time of travel, this work took me about two months.

35 *Stage 6: Completing the Union Catalogue in Cards and in Slips*

The new entries collected and the corrections made in old entries during Stage 5 should be merged with the cards and slips respectively in the Union Catalogue in Cards and in Slips.

36 *Stage 7: Preparation of the Final Press Copy*

After the work in Stage 6 is completed, the press copy for the final Union Catalogue of the country should be prepared. Whether it can be in the form of the serial numbered slips themselves or in the form of continuously typed sheets, should be determined in consultation with the printing press, and the press copy may be made accordingly (*See* Sec 3w).

37 *Stage 8: Printing and Publishing the Finalised Union Catalogue*

After Stage 7 is completed the final Union Catalogue of Learned Periodicals and Serials for India as a whole should be printed and published. Thereafter the copies should be distributed by sale or by gift, in accordance with the policy taken in this behalf.

38 *Stage 9: Preservation of the Union Catalogue in Cards*

The final Union Catalogue in Cards should be preserved in its cabinets for use during the preparation of the next edition or supplement, as the case may be, of the Union Catalogue. It should be kept up to date. At that stage the use of these cards will lead to a considerable saving in the cost of production. It will also help in the maintenance of a Uniform Standard in respect of every detail in the entries of the various editions and supplements of the Union Catalogue.

3A SOLICITING OPINION FROM THE LIBRARIANS AND USERS OF THE UNION CATALOGUE

It is helpful and necessary to solicit opinion of select librarians and users of the Union Catalogue on how it works in practice. We should also solicit suggestions, if any, for increasing the usefulness of the Union Catalogue. All the opinions and suggestions received should be recorded in a note-book and preserved for future use.

3B INDIVIDUALISING CLASS NUMBER AND RULES FOR CATALOGUING

The class numbers should be made individualising ones. For the details of making an entry the Rules given in *CCC* may be used.

3C UNIFORMISED TITLE FOR A SERIAL

The title of a Serial — particularly an administration report of a Government or of any institution — is not kept the same in all its issues. It is found that it undergoes listless unintended changes. It is not worthwhile to swell the number of entries in the Union Catalogue by giving a different Main Entry for each of its titles. It is desirable that a Standard Uniformised Title — such as "Administration report" -- may be used for all the issues of the serial considered. This need not be taken as a violation of the Canon of Ascertainability. For, that Canon does not at all stand in the way of introducing such a Uniformised Title.

3D Classified *vs* Dictionary Catalogue

It may be contended by some that a plain alphabetical list will be more helpful as a "Finding List" than a classified list, and that its cost of production also will be less. As against this the following advantages of using a classified catalogue with an alphabetical index should be considered:

1 Even as a Finding List the alphabetical index of the classified catalogue will be no less helpful, but a little more helpful than the alphabetical arrangement of the main entries; because,

11 The Title of a learned periodical or a serial can be made brief in the alphabetical part;

12 All non-substantive words — that is, auxiliary words — of the title can be suppressed wherever feasible, without loss of intelligibility;

13 The substantive words in a title can be abbreviated according to an agreed standard code of abbreviation, without loss of intelligibility;

14 Cognate words in titles in different languages can be reduced to a common abbreviation;

15 The index can be printed solid; and

16 A larger number of entries will fall in a single sweep of the eye in the alphabetical index of a classified catalogue than in the main entries of the dictionary catalogue, because in the latter each entry will occupy a few lines —

certainly more than one line. Therefore in an alphabetical catalogue a much smaller number of titles will fall within a single sweep of the eye.

2 In the classified part of the classified catalogue the prepotent element in controlling arrangement is class number. Therefore,

21 All the changes in the name of a learned periodical are brought together in their chronological sequence;

22 The learned periodicals and serials on any specific subject are entered consecutively;

23 All associated learned periodicals and serials on the same subject, issued by the same learned body, are brought together;

24 The classified arrangement of the main entries will help in rationalising the coordination of acquisition of learned periodicals and serials in the Social Sciences;

25 The classified arrangement will stimulate and be of help in bibliographical research in respect of learned periodicals and serials — particularly those of a statistical nature;

26 Such a piece of research will lay bare the subjects with no or inadequate number of learned periodicals and serials, and thus bring to the attention of research workers the fallow and near-fallow regions needing attention; and

27 The cost of preparation of a Uni-functional Alphabetical Union Catalogue will not be appreciably less than that of a Multi-functional Classified Union Catalogue.

3E Single Union Catalogue *vs* Multiple Union Catalogues

In the *Journal of documentation* 23; 1967; p 20–27 Mr M K Buckland describes an objective comparative study made by him of a single union catalogue for a country and of making several regional union catalogues. The findings of this study has been given in Sec J423.

3F Sample Page Given for a Union Catalogue

I do not now have access to learned periodicals in Social Sciences. Therefore, I am giving in Sec 3H a sample page for a Union Catalogue of Learned Periodicals in Natural Sciences.

3G Technique of Union Catalogue not Affected by Subject-Field

So far as the technique of the Union Catalogue is concerned — whether in cards or in continuous pages — the subject matter is not relevant.

3H Sample Page of the Classified Part of Union Catalogue

A″m56,K **Phil trans,** R Soc Lond.

1; 1665 C.

Index. 1: (1–70). 2: (71–110). 3: (111–120).

From 178; 1887 *continued as*

Phil trans, R Soc Lond. Ser A,

and *split partially into*

G′m56, K Phil trans, R Soc Lond. Ser B.

AH–(I)	227–230	EP–4	196, 202, 212
AV–(L)	212–219	EP–(HV–7)	171C (201)
BA–3	222, 229, 231	JD–3	1C
BK–(B)	207C (222, 231, 233)	JD–(A)	240C
BK0–(BYC)	1793 (1796, 1798–1807,1828–29,1905)	JD–(C)	178C (231–44)
BM–3	1C	JD–(HV–7)	239C
DB–4	207–234	JD–(J)	1–178
		LC–3	1C
DB–(A)	1C	LK–(L)	175–216
DB–(C)	225C		

DM-(L)	217-231	PB-3	1891-1935 (1911, 1917, 1921-29, 1931)
EB-3	1C	PL-3	1881C (1922-23)
EB-(A)	1-233 (incomplete)		
EB-(HV-7, 627)	163 C	SC-3	165-172, 216C (168)
		SC-(A)2	1C (229)
		SC-(BT)	185C
		SC-(D)	1801-36
		SC-(K)	178 C

A″m56,K,1 **Abst papers,** R Soc Lond.

1; 1800 C

Index. 1: (1-75; 1800-1905). 2: (76-130; 1905-30.)

From 5; 1843 *continued as*

Abst papers communicated R Soc.

From 7; 1855 *continued as*

Proc, R Soc Lond,

From 76; 1905 *continued as*

Proc, R Soc Lond. Series A,

and *split partially into*

G″m56,K,1 Proc, R Soc Lond. Series B.

AH-(I)	76C	FA-(M-7)	1948, 1950C
BA-3	76C(90-94)	JD-3	76C
BK-(B)	79C (113, 117, 112, 141-143, 153)	JD-(A)	192C
BKO-(BYC)	76C	JD-(C)	76C (105)
BM-3	1C (7, 29, 33, 38, 39, 50, 54, 108)	JD-(HV-7)	186C
DB-4	1C (7-10, 14-15, 25, 30, 36, 59-73, 75, 98, 158-163, 180-181, 183, 185)	JD-(J)	1C
		LC-3	1948C
DA-(A)1	148C	LK-(L)	76, 89-93 (89, 93)
DB-(A)	1C		

DB–(C)	97C	LK–(L)1	101–105
EB–3	76C (188)	PA–3	88C (100–117, 126, 137, 185, 191)
EB–(A)	48C (52,56,60–61)	PL–3	1C (138)
		QJ–(F,c)	76C
		QR–(KX,811)	93, 153–163
EB–(C)	34C (167, 170)	RC–3	1C
EB–(HV–7, 627)	76C	SC–3	1C (92–93)
EP–3	205C		
EP–(A)	174–175	SC–(A)2	80C
EP–(HV-7)	76C	SC–(D)	54–129 (75, 94–96)
		SC–(L–9U3)	76C
		SC–(Y, 72)1	193C

A″m56,K,2 **Yearbook,** R Soc Lond.

1896 C.

EP (HV–7) 1907–23 (1922)

A″m56,L **Trans,** R Soc Edin.

1; 1783 C

[1–4 published in 3 Sections].

Index. 1: (1–34; 1783–88). 2: (35–46; 1889–1908).

BM–3	1C	JD–(J)	56C (56–58)
EB–(A)	6,12–13,16,30,32,38	LC–3	1948C
EP–(HV–7)	IC (5,16,20–22, 24–26, 31)	PB–3	1788–1921
		SC–(K)	40C
		SL–(L)	1–10

A″m56,L,1 **Proc,** R Soc Edin.

1; 1832 C

[1783–1803 published in A″m56,L Transactions]

BM–3	9C	JD–(L)1	49–56
DB–(A)1	54C	LC–3	1C (61)
EB–(A)	13C	LK–(L)	31–36 (**31, 36**)
EB–(C)	31C	LK–(L)1	36–37
EB–(HV–7, 627)	46C	PB–3	44–48 (46)
EP–(HV–7)	3C (5–9, 11–12, 14)	SC–(A)2	49C
JD–3	62C	SC–(BT)	54C
JD–(A)	62C	SC–(T)	45C
JD–(C)	61C	SC–(K)	24C
JD–(J)	51C	SC–(L–9U3)	35,42–57 (**35, 43**)

A″m56,L9 **Phil mag.**

1–68; 1798–1826. ns: 1–11; 1827–32.
s3: 1–37; 1832–50. s4: 1–50; 1851–75.
s5: 1–50; 1876–1900. s6: 1–50; 1901–25.
s7: 1; 1926 C.

From 1814 *continued as*

Phil mag j,

and *amalgamated*

A″m56,L97 .J natural phil.

From 1827 *continued as*

Phil mag or An chem, math, astro, nat hist gen sc.

From 1832 *continued as*

Lond Edin phil mag j sc,

and *amalgamated*

A″m56,M24 Edin j sc

From 1841 *continued as*

Lond Edin Dubl phil mag j sc.

From 1945 *continued as*

Phil mag, j theor expt applied phys.

AV–(L)	s7: 9–12	EP–3	s7: 42C
BA–3	s6: 15C (s6: 21–23, 39–45)	EP–4	s6: 27–s7:15
BM–3	s6: 15C	EP–(HV–7)	s4: 1C
CT–3	s7: 17–18	JD–3	s7: 18C
DB–(A)	1813C (1820–31)	JD–(C)	s7: 43C
		SC–3	s6: 14C
DB–(C)	1888C	LC–3	s7: 38C
EB–(A)	s6: 21C (s6: 26, 32–38)	PB–3	1C (s6: : 11
EB–(C)	s7: 38C	PL–3	s5: 1C (s5: 14–15)
EB–(HV–7, 627)	s6: 31C	SC–(D)	s5: 33–s7: 28

3J TABLE 1: SAMPLE CODE NUMBER OF LIBRARIES

The following is the key to the Code Numbers for the libraries used in the holdings sections in the sample page of a Classified Part of a Union Catalogue:

SN	Code Number	Meaning of Code Number
1	AH-3	Andhra Pradesh, Hyderabad, Osmania University Library
2	AH-(I)	—, —, Library of Department of Botany of Osmania University
3	AT-3	—, Tirupathi, Venkateswara University Library
4	AV-(L)	—, Visakapatnam, Andhra Medical College Library
5	AW-3	—, Waltair, Andhra University Library
6	BA-3	Tamil Nadu, Annamalainagar, Annamalai University Library
7	BK-(B)	—, Karaikudi, Indian Mathematical Society, Ramanujan Institute Library
8	BKO-(BYC)	—, Kodaikanal, Solar Observatory Library
9	BM-3	—, Madras, Madras University Library
10	BMA-3	—, Madurai, Madurai University Library
11	CC-3	Kerala, Calicut, Calicut University Library
12	CT-3	—, Trivandrum, Kerala University Library
13	DB-4	Mysore, Bangalore, Central College Library
14	DB-(A)1	—, —, Indian Academy of Science Library
15	DB-(C)	—, —, Raman Institute Library
16	DM-(L)	—, Mysore (city), Medical College Library
17	EB-3	Maharashtra, Bombay, Bombay University Library
18	EB-(A)	—, —, Institute of Science Library
19	EB-(C)	—, —, Tata Institute of Fundamental Research Library
20	EB-(HV-7, 627)	—, —, Alibag and Magnetic Observatories
21	EP-3	—, Poona, Poona University Library
22	EP-4	—, —, Bai Jerabai Wadia Library, Fergusson College
23	EP-(A)	—, —, Maharashtra Association for the Cultivation of Science Library
24	EP-(HV-7)	—, —, Meteorological Office Library
25	FA-(M-7)	Gujarat, Ahmedabad Textile Industry's Research Association Library
26	JD-3	Delhi, University of Delhi Library
27	JD-(A)	—, National Institute of Sciences Library

SN	Code Number	Meaning or Code Number
28	JD-(C)	—, National Physical Laboratory Library
29	JD-(J)	—, Indian Agricultural Research Institute Library
30	JD-(HV-7)	—, Director General of Observatories Libraries
31	JD-(L)1	—, Malarial Institute of India, Library
32	LC-3	—, Punjab, Chandigarh University Library
33	LK-(L)	—, Kasauli, Indian Council of Medical Research Library
34	LK-(L;41)	—, —, Central Research Institute Library
35	MS-3	Kashmir, Srinagar, Kashmir University Library
36	PA-3	Uttar Pradesh, Aligarh, Aligarh Muslim University
37	PAL-3	—, Allahabad, Allahabad University Library
38	PB-3	—, Banaras, Banaras Hindu University Library
39	PL-3	—, Lucknow, University Library
40	QJ-(F,c)	Bihar, Jamshedpur, Tata Iron and Steel Co., New Control and Research Laboratory Library
41	QR-(KX, 811)	—, Ranchi, Indian Lac Research Institute Library
42	RC-3	Orissa, Cuttack, Utkal University Library
43	SC-3	West Bengal, Calcutta, Calcutta University Library
44	SC-31	—, —, Jadavpur University Library
45	SC-(A)	—, —, Bose Research Institute Library
46	SC-(A)1	—, —, Indian Association for the Cultivation of Science Library
47	SC-(BT)	—, —, Indian Statistical Institute Library
48	SC-(D)	—, —, Bengal Engineering College Library
49	SC-(E)	—, —, Indian Chemical Society Library
50	SC-(K)	—, —, Zoological Survey of India Library
51	SC-(L)	—, —, Calcutta Medical College Library
52	SC-(L-9U3)	—, —, School of Tropical Medicine Library
53	SC-(Y, 72)1	—, —, Library of Department of Anthropology of Indian Museum
54	UG-3	Assam, Gauhati, Gauhati University Library

3K ADVANTAGE OF THE USE OF CODE NUMBERS IN THE HOLDING SECTION

The Code Numbers for libraries have been so designed as to facilitate any library, needing an inter-library loan, easily locating the nearest library capable of helping it. Here are two illustrations:

1 According to Sec M3H, in the Union Catalogue the Library with the Code Number PA–3 (= Aligarh Muslim University Library in UP) does not have the *Philosophical transactions* of the Royal Society of London. Suppose one of its readers wants a volume of it. Its librarian puts his finger, as it were, on the Code Number of his library—PA–3. He scans the Code Numbers of the libraries having *Philosophical transactions*. He finds that the *Philosophical transactions* are available in the following libraries:

PB–3 (UP, Banaras Hindu University Library)

PL–3 (UP, Lucknow University Library); and

JD–3 (Delhi University Library).

From his local knowledge of relative distance he knows that out of these three libraries Delhi is nearer to him. Therefore he applies to Delhi University Library for the inter-library loan.

2 The Code Number PAL–3 (= Allahabad University Library) does not have the *Philosophical transactions* of the Royal Society of London. Suppose one of its readers wants a volume of it. Its librarian puts his finger, as it were, on the Code Number of his library—PAL–3. He finds that the *Philosophical transactions* are available in the following libraries:

PB–3 (= Banaras Hindu University Library); and

PL–3 (= Lucknow University Library)

From his local knowledge of relative distance he knows that out of these two libraries, Banaras is nearer to him. Therefore he applies to Banaras Hindu University Library for inter-library loan.

Thus, inter-library loan of a volume of any learned periodical for the use of a specialist reader or for reprographic work, can be managed bilaterally between two libraries in a most economical way. There will be no need to bring in the national documentation centre as a third party. Nor will there be need for a library to write to several libraries to find out the library that can help it. The only work to be done by a national documentation centre will be to arrange for inter-library loan with libraries in foreign countries.

3M STRUCTURE OF THE CODE NUMBERS FOR A LIBRARY

The Code Number of a library represents the library in terms of

1 Its Constituent State (for the code numbers of Constituent States see the table in Sec 3N. For an alphabetical index to the code number of the Constituent States see the table in Sec 3P);

2 Its Locality (for an alphabetical index of the localities see the table in Sec 3Q);

3 Its Status, if it is a generalist library (for the code numbers for the different kinds of generalist libraries see table in Sec 3S and for an alphabetical index to the code numbers of the different kinds of generalist libraries see table in Sec 3T); or

4 Its Subject of Specialisation if it is a specialist library (for the Colon Code Numbers for the subjects see table in Sec 3U); and

5 An Indo-Arabic numeral added after the Code Number got by categories 1 to 4 in case two or more libraries otherwise get the same code numbers. (For examples see Sec 3J).

3N TABLE 2: CODE NUMBERS FOR THE CONSTITUENT STATES, UNION TERRITORIES, AND SIMILAR OTHER TRACTS

The following table arranges the Constituent States of India according to the Principle of Spatial Contiguity and each State is given a Code Number accordingly. The Code Number for a Constituent State is a Roman cap.

A Andhra Pradesh	M Kashmir
B Tamil Nadu (including Pondicherry)	N Himachal Pradesh
C Kerala	P Uttar Pradesh
D Mysore	Q Bihar
E Maharashtra (including Goa)	R Orissa
F Gujarat	S West Bengal
G Madhya Pradesh	T Meghalaya
H Rajasthan	U Assam
J Delhi	V Arunachala Pradesh
K Haryana	W Nagaland
L Punjab	X Manipur
	Y Mizoram
	Z Tripura

3P TABLE 3: ALPHABETICAL INDEX TO CODE NUMBERS FOR THE CONSTITUENT STATES, UNION TERRITORIES, AND OTHER SIMILAR TRACTS

Andhra Pradesh A	Manipur X
Arunachala Pradesh V	Meghalaya T
Assam U	Mizoram Y
Bihar Q	Mysore D
Delhi J	Nagaland W
Goa E	Orissa R
Gujarat F	Pondicherry B
Haryana K	Punjab L
Himachal Pradesh N	Rajasthan H
Kashmir M	Tamil Nadu B
Kerala C	Tripura Z
Madhya Pradesh G	Uttar Pradesh P
Maharashtra E	West Bengal S

3Q TABLE 4: ALPHABETICAL INDEX TO CODE NUMBERS FOR THE LOCALITIES

SN	Name of the Locality	Code N	SN	Name of the Locality	Code N
1	Ahmedbad	FA	16	Karaikudi	BK
2	Aligarh	PA	17	Kasauli	LK
3	Allahabad	PAL	18	Kodaikanal	BK
4	Annamalainagar	BA	19	Lucknow	PL
5	Banaras	PB	20	Madras	BM
6	Bangalore	DB	21	Madurai	BMA
7	Bombay	EB	22	Mysore (city)	DM
8	Calcutta	SC	23	Poona	EP
9	Calicut	CC	24	Ranchi	QR
10	Chandigarh	LC	25	Srinagar	MS
11	Cuttack	RC	26	Tirupathi	AT
12	Delhi	JD	27	Trivandrum	CT
13	Gauhati	UG	28	Visakapatnam	AV
14	Hyderabad	AH	29	Waltair	AW
15	Jamshedpur	QJ			

3R LOCALITIES OF THE SAME STATE, BEGINNING WITH THE SAME LETTER

Consider the items 20 and 21 in the table in Sec 3Q. They read,

Madras	BM
Madurai	BMA

The names of both these localities begin with the same letter "M". Therefore, the use of this letter alone will not individualise them. The following convention is adopted to individualise them. For what may be regarded as the more important locality, from the point of view of the libraries, we use the first letter alone to represent it. For the locality second in order, we use the first two letters, to individualise it. If another locality also has to be individualised with a letter-pair as in Madurai, we differentiate their locality by using the first three letters. It should be remembered that this device will be necessary only to individualise localities within one and the same State.

3S TABLE 5: CODE NUMBER FOR THE KINDS OF STATUS OF GENERALIST LIBRARIES

SN	Code N	Status	SN	Code N	Status
1	1	State Central Library	4	4	College Library
2	2	Public Library	5	5	School Library
3	3	University Library	6	6	Museum Library

3T TABLE 6: ALPHABETICAL INDEX TO CODE NUMBERS FOR THE KINDS OF STATUS OF GENERALIST LIBRARIES

SN	Status	Code N	SN	Status	Code N
1	College Library	4	4	School Library	5
2	Museum Library	6	5	State Central Library	1
3	Public Library	2	6	University Library	3

3U TABLE 7: COLON CODE NUMBERS FOR DIFFERENT SUBJECTS

SN	Code N	Subject	SN	Code N	Subject
1	(A)	Natural Science (General)	11	(I)	Botany
2	(B)	Mathematics	12	(J)	Agriculture
3	(BT)	Statistical Calculus	13	(K)	Zoology
4	(BYC)	Astrophysics	14	(KX, 811)	Lac
5	(C)	Physics	15	(L)	Medicine
6	(D)	Engineering	16	(L; 41)	Infectious Disease
7	(E)	Chemistry	17	(L-9UA3)	Tropical Medicine
8	(F,C)	Iron and Steel	18	M-7	Textile
9	(HV-7)	Meteorology	19	(Y, 72)	Anthropology
10	(HV-7, 627)	Magnetic Meteorology			

For other Social Sciences *See* Sec 2d.

3V Alphabetical Index to the Colon Code Numbers for Different Subjects

Agriculture (J)
Anthropology (Y, 72)
Astrophysics (BYC)
Botany (I)
Chemistry (E)
Engineering (D)
Infectious Disease (L;41)
Iron and Steel (F,c)
Lac (KX, 811)
Magnetic Meteorology (HV-7, 627)
Mathematics (B)
Medicine (L)
Meteorology (HV-7)
Natural Science (A)
Physics (C)
Statistical Calculus (BT)
Textile (M-7)
Tropical Medicine (L-9U3)
Zoology (K)

3W Delegation of the Responsibility of Union Catalogue to Different National Service Libraries

As and when National Service Libraries are established for two or more subject-fields and they put on full steam, the responsibility for the preparation, publication, and the maintenance of the Union Catalogue should be handed over to the National Service Library concerned.

3X Social Science Periodicals in Indian Languages

Of late, periodicals — weeklies, monthlies etc, and newspapers — published in an Indian language — are carrying articles worth inclusion in the Union Catalogue of Social Science Periodical Publications. Further, newspapers in Indian languages — and sometimes even periodicals in such languages — contain news-items not found in similar English publications of India. Therefore, the time will soon come to include them in the Union Catalogue. This raises some issues:

1 Should we make a separate Union Catalogue for each language; or

2 Can we make a common Union Catalogue for all languages sharing the same script;

3 Should we make a common Union Catalogue for all the languages using transliteration into Devanagari Script, more widely used among the Indian languages than any other Indian script;

4 Should we produce a single Union Catalogue of all periodicals and serials irrespective of their respective languages;

5 In case of Category 4 being preferred, should the translated-into script be Roman or Devanagari;

6 In case of Category 5 being preferred, should we give after the name of the periodical or serial in the transcribed form, the title in its own language.

These problems will arise in the Social Sciences much earlier than in the Natural Sciences. But merging all the entries into one sequence by using transliteration into one script may involve difficulties in printing. For, it may be difficult to print in the same volume entries having lines in different scripts.

4 Wrong Functions of the Insodoc

The following functions enumerated in Appendix VII of the *Annual report*, 2, 1970-71 of the ICSSR do not belong to the Insodoc:

"(3) **Library:** The Documentation Centre will maintain a specialised library. It will not try to acquire books in social sciences as such, except in some small and highly specialised fields such as research methodology. Its principal holdings will be in terms of social science serials [Periodical Publications]. Here also, care will be taken to see that holdings which are readily available in other libraries in Delhi are not duplicated. Emphasis will be placed on the collection of microfilm and microfiche materials. The specific character of the collection will emerge in the course of the development of the Centre in the first few years. One thing, however, can be said definitely. The holdings of the Documentation Centre will be planned to supplement the national resources available in the field of social sciences rather than for duplicating the stocks which already exist.

"(4) **Doctoral Theses in Social Sciences:** The Council has taken up a programme of collecting a synopsis (of about 5,000 words) of every Ph D thesis in the field of Social Sciences approved by Indian Universities from their inception up to 31 December 1969. It is estimated that there are about 3,000 such theses. These synopses will be maintained for reference in the Documentation Centre and made available to research scholars. With effect from 1st January 1970, universities are requested to send one copy of every doctoral thesis approved by them in the field of Social Sciences to the Documentation Centre. A majority of them have agreed to do so and the matter is being pursued with others. The Council hopes that the Documentation Centre will soon have one copy of every doctoral thesis approved by every Indian University in the field of Social Sciences (or its synopsis) which could be made available to scholars for reference. Needless to say, this will be a unique collection and service which the Documentation Centre will be able to provide.

"(6) **Data Libraries:** Similarly, the Council has also decided to establish a network of data libraries in different social science fields. They will be located in selected institutions and assisted by the Council. They will also maintain a certain uniformity in the data collected. At the apex of this system, there will be a National Data Library, which will coordinate the work of all the data libraries in the country and also supplement their resources. This apex unit will be an integral part of the National Documentation Centre.

"(11) **Repository Function:** The Documentation Centre will develop a repository function in respect of old volumes of social science serials which it will accept for deposit from all collaborating libraries. It will hold them in trust on their behalf, maintain them in good condition and make them available to all research scholars.

Note.—

1 Each of the above functions amounts to the maintenance by the Insodoc of a library of one kind or another.

2 Each such library may have to be used by the Insodoc, as need arises;

3 But the development and the maintenance of any such library should not be taken up by the Insodoc itself; for the function of Insodoc is entirely different from the function of a library.

4 Each of the libraries mentioned in this section should form a unit of the system of national libraries to be maintained by the Government of India according to Sec 62 of Schedule 7 (Union List) of the *Constitution of India* (1949).

5 In view of the likelihood of need arising for Insodoc consulting such libraries, all that is wanted is that the Insodoc should be situated adjacent to or in close proximity of the libraries concerned.

5 Right Delegation of Function

As and when the quantum of work in the Insodoc increases beyond a convenient measure, the right course would be to replace an omnibus Documentation Centre for all Social Sciences by a separate national documentation centre for each specified subject field among social sciences. The need for this may not arise in the near future, at least not in the next decade. Therefore I am not now going to the reasons for some entries having to be repeated in two or more national documentation lists prepared by the different national documentation centres in Social Sciences. Nor do I describe at this stage the way in which the different national documentation centres in Social Sciences should consult with one another for mutually helping one another in finding out the seepage of papers relevant to the particular list and appearing in a learned periodical, falling predominantly within the subject field of some other national documentation centre.

6 Wrong Delegation of Function

61 Proposed Delegation to Specialised Institutions

The *Annual report,* 2, 1970-71 of the ICSSR, Appendix VII, page 121, states that "The Council proposes to set up a National Bibliographical and Documentation Service. Under this programme, institutions will be selected in different parts of the country to do bibliographical and documentation work in specified fields for which they have special competence and facilities. For instance, the Indian Society of Agricultural Economics will be requested to do the bibliographical and documentation work in the field of agricultural economics. The Anthropological Survey of India will do a similar service in the field of anthropology."

62 Specialised Nature of Documentation Work Not Realised

The programme mentioned in Sec 61 looks amateurish. It does not show a knowledge of the need for specialised techniques to do Documentation Work. If the intention is to appoint documentalists in each of these centres, it will lead to avoidable expense due to duplication of staff and work. This is a result of not knowing of the primary function of National Documentation Centre being the production of an advance national documentation list.

63 Division of Labour Forgotten

In making the specialist research workers in the different learned societies such as those mentioned in the *Annual report* to do the Documentation Work, three important factors are ignored:

1 The specialist research worker does know the subject very well. But he does not know the specialities of Documentation Work;

2 Nor is it conducive to national economy to make him learn these specialities. The purpose of the formation of a separate profession of documentalists, during the last two decades, has been to allow the research workers to devote their full time to research work, instead of spending part of the time in documentation work, without prejudice to the mutual consultation between documentalists and specialist research workers as and when need arises for it.

3 This implies a wholesome division of labour between the profession of documentalists on the one hand and the profession of research workers on the other. To overlook the importance of such a division of labour is to go back by several centuries in the economic organisation and utilisation of man-power.

64 Experience in the West

The countries of the West realised the importance of documentation work, about five decades ago. On the downpour of research papers beginning to approach a million in a year, the library profession of the West had been confining itself to the needs of public libraries and generalist readers. They had not equipped themselves to meet the needs of specialist libraries and of research workers. Nor did they realise the national need for equipping themselves for documentation work. Therefore, some of the research workers themselves had to be forced to spend part of their research time in doing documentation work. But, after World War II the library profession slowly realised its new function of serving specialist readers in the present day conditions. Then they began to develop proper techniques of documentation. In due course, the research workers found it useful to withdraw themselves from documentation work.

65 Regional Delegation

It is wrong and unhelpful to delegate the functions of the Insodoc to regional documentation centres. It will lead to duplication of work and increase in cost without any advantage. But, this kind of regional delegation has been prescribed in Appendix VII of the *Annual report*, 2, 1970-71, of the ICSSR, in the following words:

"In addition to Social Science Documentation Centre at New Delhi, the Council should also establish some Regional Centres. A beginning should be made, during the next three years, by establishing Centres at a few selected regional centres. However, it would be necessary, over the next few years, to develop a Centre in each State or at least for each linguistic region."

This wrong idea is traceable to the failure to recognise the primary function of the national documentation centre being that of producing an advance documentation periodical of an exhaustive kind.

66 Misunderstanding about the Function of a Documentation Centre

The following passage occurring in page 124, in Appendix VII of the *Annual report*, 2, 1970-71 of the ICSSR, implies a misunderstanding of the function of a national documentation centre — and mixing it up with the function of a service library, which will have its own documentalists for doing documentation service to readers:

"(*a*) The Centres may provide facilities to social scientists, especially those working in colleges in the mofussil areas, to refresh themselves or to improve their professional competence by availing themselves of the library and other facilities which may be available at these Centres. It may be necessary to institute a system of financial awards for this purpose to cover the travel and other costs involved.

"(b) They may maintain bibliographical and documentation services which would be of use to the researchers.

"(c) They may also maintain a good library of serials (no attempt should be made to build up collection of books) and facilities for using microfilm copies, etc.

"(d) They may hold summer schools in social sciences and training courses in research methodology.

"(e) They may organise seminars and discussions among social scientists and also try to bring together social scientists who are actively engaged in research.

"(f) They may collect social science research materials in the regional languages, with special reference to the areas served by each Centre, in collaboration with other institutions engaged in similar work which might also be financially supported to develop their aproved programmes in the field. The Centres may also act as agents of the

ICSSR in collecting information and materials for its programmes.

"(g) They may also maintain, if necessary, a good hostel where social scientists (university teachers, teachers of affiliated colleges or Ph D students in social sciences and other research workers in the field) can stay at a minimal cost."

7 Hope

71 Avoidance of Mistake

The following is the hope:

1 All the wrong functions proposed to be given to the Insodoc will be given up.

2 The well known difference between the work of a national documentation centre and documentation service to readers will be borne in mind, and will not be mixed up; and

3 Documentation service can be done only by a service library making it possible for documentalist and the reader meeting in the presence of the documents themselves, their catalogue entries, and the documentation lists available in the library.

72 Right Functions Alone from the Very Beginning

The provision for a National Documentation Centre for Social Sciences is being made in India for the first time. The increase in research in Social Sciences is becoming imperative for policy-making by the Governments in the country. And research in social sciences is also being taken up by the universities and research institutions in an increasing measure. The departments of the Government will also have to play a part in this matter:

1 In finding out the problems of research;

2 In communicating them to the research organisations; and

3 In testing the helpfulness or otherwise of the results of research.

These form the wish about the work and the organisation of the Insodoc.

CHAPTER M

INDIAN ASSOCIATION OF SPECIAL LIBRARIES AND INFORMATION CENTRES

1 Genesis

11 Attempt 1: Not Pursued

On 21 January 1949, the second day of the All India Library Conference (8) (Nagpur), Dr G T Kale, Librarian of the Indian Institute of Science (Bangalore) moved that a Special Libraries Association be formed. According to him this idea had been commended by Miss Ditmas, the then Director of the Aslib (=Association of Special Libraries and Information Bureaux) (U K). As President, I observed that,

1 A courtesy reply received from Miss Ditmas need not be cited as the reason for the proposal;

2 The subject should be considered on its own merits in the Indian context;

3 Only some of the members of the Indian Library Association could become members of the proposed Specialist Libraries Association also;

4 Any paper on any problem of specialist libraries could be given due weight for inclusion in the Organ of the Indian Library Association;

5 There was (at that time) hardly any specialist library in India facing any problem different from those faced by University Libraries; and

6 The University Libraries and the Government of India libraries contributed the largest number to the Indian Library Association. After some discussion, the mover agreed to draft a constitution for the proposed Association

for consideration by the Council of the Indian Library Association. But no draft constitution was furnished by him.

12 Attempt 2: Successful

In 1955, another Attempt was made to establish a Specialist Libraries Association. At that time, the initiative was taken by J Saha (Librarian, Indian Statistical Institute), A K Mukherjee (Librarian, Department of Anthropology, Indian Museum), and G B Ghosh (Librarian, Geological Survey of India). They all belonged to Calcutta. After an informal discussion among themselves in May 1955, they explained their proposal to Dr H L Hora (Director, Zoological Survey of India, Calcutta) and got his enthusiastic support. They also got the support of Prof P C Mahalanobis, Dr D M Bose, Dr J C Ghosh, Dr H J Bhabha and others. Ultimately, at a meeting held on 3 September 1955 at the Lecture Hall of the Indian Museum (Calcutta) the Association was formed with the name "Indian Association of Special Libraries and Information Centres" — shortened name "Iaslic." This was the genesis of the Iaslic.

2 Objectives of the Iaslic

21 Objectives Laid Down by the Constitution

In 1956, the Iaslic outlined its objectives as follows:

1 Encouraging and promoting the systematic acquisition, organisation, and dissemination of knowledge;

2 Promoting the improvement of quality of library and information services and documentation work;

3 Coordinating the activities of and fostering mutual cooperation and assistance among, the special libraries, scientific, technological, and research institutions, learned

societies, commercial organizations, industrial research establishments, as well as other information and documentation centres, to the fullest extent;

4 Serving as a forum of active contact for libraries, information bureaux, documentation centres, scientists, research workers, specialists, and others having common interest;

5 Promoting improvement of technical efficiency of the workers in specialist libraries and information and documentation centres, and looking after their professional welfare;

6 Promoting centres of research in specialist library and documentation techniques;

7 Acting as a centre of information in scientific, technical and other fields; and

8 Taking all such actions as may be incidental or conducive to the attainment of the objects of the Association, or any of them.

22 Divisions of the Iaslic

For performing the functions mentioned in Sec 21 the Iaslic has the following divisions, as mentioned in its Constitution:

1 Documentation;
2 Education;
3 Publication and Publicity;
4 Library and Information Service;
5 Reprography and Translation; and
6 Cooperation and Coordination of libraries.

3 Remarks on the Points Mentioned in Sec 2

31 Remarks on the Constitutional Objectives

1 "Encouraging and promoting the systematic acquisition, organisation, and dissemination of knowledge" is a common objective of all library associations. This objective emphasises only "Encouragement and Promotion." This is but right. For, a privately managed association cannot itself do all that needs to be done. It can only encourage and promote them.

2 "Promoting the improvement of quality of library and information services and documentation work" is a right objective. The reasons for this are the same as those given in support of objective 1.

3 "Coordinating the activities of and fostering mutual cooperation and assistance among, the special libraries, scientific, technological, and research institutions, learned societies, commercial organisations, as well as other information and documentation centres, to the fullest extent" is without doubt a correct and distinctive objective of an Association of Specialist Libraries. As already stated in Chap D, service by specialist libraries is something new in the history of libraries driving home the most economical way of organising specialist libraries and their service during these early years is essential.

4 "Serving as a forum of active contact for libraries, information bureaux, documentation centres, scientists, research workers, specialists, and others having common interest" is but one of the means for carrying out objective 3. Therefore this object is also, without doubt, a correct, distinctive and primary objective.

5 "Promoting improvement of technical efficiency of the workers in specialist libraries and information and

documentation centres, and looking after their professional welfare" is a second means for carrying out the primary objective mentioned in category 3. Thus this is also a correct objective.

6 "Promoting centres of research in specialist library and documentation techniques" is only a third means for carrying out the primary objective mentioned in category 3. Thus, this is also a correct objective.

7 "Acting as a centre of information in scientific, technical and other fields" is also a means for carrying out the primary objective mentioned in category 3. But, the carrying out of this objective may land the Iaslic in financial and man-power requirements beyond its capacity. This must be avoided. To avoid this, this objective should, by convention, be interpreted carefully so as to keep it within the financial and man-power capacity of the Iaslic.

8 "Taking all such actions as may be incidental or conducive to the attainment of the objects of the Association, or any of them" is but a usual statement to take freedom to take up new unforeseen objectives.

4 Wrong Functions

41 TRAINING OF DOCUMENTALISTS

1 A part-time six-month course was given to Dip Lib Sc's and B Lib Sc's in 1966-67. The Course was called "Training in Special Librarianship and Documentation." As judged by the name of the Course and by the fact of 10 senior librarians having been teachers during the course completed in about 150 days, perhaps it was meant to be a systematic professional course for documentalists. If so, the standard of the course should have been somewhat low — certainly much lower than that of the DRTC Course. If it be so, this was a wrong function of the Iaslic. It should have known of the existence of the Documentation Re-

search and Training Centre (DRTC), Bangalore, and of the optional subject of Documentation being taught in the M Lib Sc course of some University, and should have abstained from taking up this wrong function.

2 From 1967 to 1970, the duration of the course was extended to one year. In spite of the extension of the duration of the Course, all the remarks made under category 1 hold good, in this case also.

3 Waiting for the recognition of the Course by the Government, the Course was suspended in 1970.

411 *Disservice to Iaslic's Mission*

Giving a lower standard of training in Documentation — lower than that of DRTC — and putting these trainees into market as specialist librarians and documentalists may work against the good intentions of the Iaslic. For,

1 Without having designed a depth schedule for some select subject, and having practised abstracting work as part of the assignment during the course of training and in association with it, as in DRTC (this is spread over about seven months during the course itself and about six months in the post-training period), the candidate may not be able to meet the specific requirements of the specialist library appointing him;

2 After appointing a candidate of a lower standard of training, the employers will form a wrong and poor impression of documentation work and service;

3 The employers have not yet understood the true helpful function of a documentalist; and

4 The poor performance of the candidate will militate against the profession of documentalists in getting the respect, the status, and the scale of salary worthy of the profession.

The Iaslic is requested to examine the points mentioned above before reviving the Course suspended in 1970.

42 PART-TIME COURSE IN RUSSIAN

The following information is culled out from the Annual Reports of the Iaslic:

Year	N of Students	
	Admitted	Took the Examination
1958	27	5
1959	12	4
1960	14	4

For want of students, the course was discontinued since 1961. The Iaslic itself has thus realised that this was a wrong function for it.

43 PART-TIME COURSE IN GERMAN

The following information is culled out from the Annual Reports of the Iaslic:

Year	N of Students	
	Admitted	Took the Examination
1958	30	10
1959	35	6
1960	6	0
1961	13	4
1962	15	4
1963	12	0

Perhaps, as in the case of the Russian Course, the German Course also has been suspended since 1963.

44 REMARKS ON THE LANGUAGE COURSE

Evidently, the courses in Russian and German were conducted by the Iaslic to produce translators for Specialist Libraries. But, they have proved a failure. Surely, the Iaslic should have now been convinced that this was a wrong function for them to take up. Even Universities find it difficult to give the right kind of course in a foreign language for translators. The training of translators should be diversified on the basis of language *cum* subject combination. A competent translator should acquire not only proficiency in the translated-from language and in the translated-into language, but also a workable knowledge of the subject field — particularly of the technical terms in it. Even Universities find it difficult to get such candidates for training. I have observed this experience in many European countries. I have had a full discussion about the difficulties in this, with the Authorities of the Humboldt University, East Berlin.

45 Reprography Service

The following information is culled out from the Annual Reports of the Iaslic:

Year	Microfilm copy	Copy of readable size	Year	Microfilm copy	Copy of readable size
1958	20,000	1,270	1965	55,004	2,297
1959	25,051	1,306	1966	62,729	2,422
1960	40,278	2,420	1967	72,002	2,638
1961	48,687	3,935	1968	—	—
1962	49,001	1,899	1969	14,213	769
1963	50,019	1,913	1970	12,263	419
1964	54,000	2,000			
			Total	503,247	23,288

The supply of about 500,000 microfilm copies and about 23,000 readable-size photocopies should have involved a total turnover of about Rs 150,000. Such a function should not be taken up by a learned or a promotional body consisting of honorary workers. The Iaslic should consider abandoning this wrong function. In this connection attention is invited to Sec K3c.

46 Translation Service

Practically all the remarks given in Sec M45 are applicable to Translation Service also.

47 Publication of *Indian library science abstracts*

Iaslic started the publication of the *Indian library science abstracts* in 1967. But all the four issues of Vol 2 (1968) had to be brought out as a single one in 1972. The same was the case with Vol 3 (1969). This proves the arduous and the difficult nature of work of this kind for an association with honorary workers. On the other hand, the Insdoc is publishing a bare index without abstracts of the Indian papers on Library Science. The latter is virtually a governmental body. In this context, it is desirable that the Iaslic and the Insdoc come to an understanding on this subject so that the Iaslic is relieved of this difficult function; and at any rate, there should be no duplication of efforts in this country.

471 *Comparison of the Output of the Non-Governmental Iaslic and of the Governmental Insdoc*

The following comparative table of the number of papers covered by the list published by the Iaslic, a non-governmental body, and the Insdoc, a governmental body, should be carefully considered.

Year	Iaslic	Insdoc
1967	372	976
1968	242	1,032
1969	275	768

The greater number of entries in the Insdoc list should be due to its covering foreign papers also. The Iaslic should persuade the Insdoc to provide abstracts to each entry — not merely the synopsis of authors as the Iaslic does. A paper by S Seetharama and myself entitled "Slimming the abstract of a paper: Symbiosis between the subject heading within a main entry and the abstract" and published as Paper AA in the Volume of Papers of the DRTC Seminar (9) (1971) has shown how a full informative abstract can be made quite slim and yet fully informative in a classified arrangement of entries.

5 Right Functions of the Iaslic

Some of the functions mentioned in Sec M4 and taken up by the Iaslic might have appeared to be right functions in the conditions prevailing in the country in the early years of the Iaslic. But, they do not seem to be either necessary or right functions in the present context. Iaslic can do a good service to the wing of the library profession working in specialist libraries, by its confining itself to the functions described in the following sub-sections.

51 Publication of the *Iaslic bulletin*: Analysis of Papers Published upto 1970

Particulars	Total	Papers on			
		Public relation work in specialist libraries	Documentation techniques	Library science general	Outside library science
Total	191	62	25	90	14
Percentage	100	32	13	48	7

1 The category "outside library science" includes papers such as

1 "General committee on public instruction in the early English schools in India"; and

2 "Study of the alphabet."

A paper on subjects such as these should not be admitted by the Iaslic.

2 The category "Library science, general" includes papers such as

1 "Trend and progress of public library development in India"; and

2 "Library profession: Its status and function."

Perhaps the reason for including such papers pertaining to Library Science in general is that the Indian Library Association is not bringing out its periodical regularly, but it is desirable that the Iaslic leaves the publication of such papers to the Library Science periodicals of a general nature, current in India.

3 The analysis of the 25 papers on documentation techniques gives the following results:

Particulars	Standard 1	Standard 2	Standard 3	Total
N of papers	5	16	4	25
Percentage	20	64	16	100

4 It is desirable that the Iaslic leaves the publication of the papers of standard 1 on "documentation techniques" to the *Library science with a slant to documentation* or to the *Annals of library science and documentation*. The papers of standards 2 and 3 are quite suitable to the *Iaslic bulletin*, particularly if they have plenty of case studies by way of illustration. These papers will be more helpful if they are not rehashes of ideas described by others, but if they embody the ideas developed by the members of the Iaslic in their Study Circles (*See* Sec M57).

5 The papers of the category "Public relation work" are of the most appropriate ones. Most of the pages of the *Iaslic bulletin* should be occupied by this kind of papers.

52 PERSUASION OF INDUSTRIAL AND COMMERCIAL ENTERPRISES

In the *Iaslic bulletin,* there should be many papers setting forth the benefits—particularly the financial benefit—flowing to the industrial and commercial enterprises from the documentation work and service given by their respective specialist libraries. Some may be theoretical but many should be case studies. The Iaslic should continuously collect and publish such case studies from the industrial and commercial enterprises of foreign countries as well as of India. It should be the distinctive and primary function of the Iaslic. For this reason, the *Iaslic bulletin* should give the largest possible space to them.

53 PERSUASION OF THE GOVERNMENT DEPARTMENTS

In the *Iaslic bulletin* there should be many papers, with a large number of case studies, setting forth the benefits of documentation work and service given to the Departments of Government, by their respective departmental libraries; one form of benefit being, decisions of a Government on the problems engaging their attention from time to time, basing not merely on the precedence contained in the office files, but on the latest theories and practices being developed on the problems in the different countries of the world.

531 *Anecdote About a Department of the Union Government*

A few years ago a senior officer of the Home Ministry collected information from DRTC for organising the library of that Department as a specialist library doing documentation work and giving documentation service. But, his proposal received only partial approval of his Department! (*See* Sec d92). This emphasises the need for the members of the Iaslic doing a considerable amount of lobbying work among Government Departments not only in Delhi but also in the capitals of all the Constituent States.

532 *Anecdote on the Opposition of a Government Secretary to Documentation Service*

Even the suggestion of the benefits of documentation service to the Department of a Government is resented by some Government Secretaries. (*See* Sec d4 to d91). This shows the need for turning the attention of the Iaslic on the problem of persuading the Officers of the Government Departments to accept documentation work and service. This too will have to be done with the Officers, not only of the Union Government but also of the Government of each of the Constituent States.

533 *Anecdote of Plenipotentiary Work to be Used as a Model for Iaslic*

In another instance, an old student of mine, in the Mathematics Department of the Presidency College, Madras, before my taking charge of the Madras University Library in 1924, was the Chairman of the Central Board of Revenue. The librarian of the Board was also an old student of mine when I was teaching library science in the University of Madras. I happened to step into the room of the Chairman one day.

SRR.—Do you take the help of your librarian in your official work?

Chairman.—No. My work is very specialised. How can the librarian be of any help to me?

SRR.—Shall I demonstrate to you not only the possibility but also the necessity for taking the help from the librarian?

Chairman.—You are an exception. I remember Sir Maurice Gwyer describing you as a "Prince among librarians."

SRR.—Any librarian can give you adequate library service (we now call it Documentation Service in order to take away the old equation of a librarian with a library attender). He need not be a "Prince"! Did you ever give a chance to your librarian?

Chairman.—No, Sir.

SRR.—Can you recognise him?

Chairman (with laughter).—I am sorry, I cannot. I have never seen him.

SRR.—Let me demonstrate how he can help you. Push on to me the file on the top of the heap on your table. (After a perusal) This is on double taxation. A glance through the file shows that most of the sheets are meandering among the same old outmoded ideas, found in a succession of office notes, quoting precedent after precedent in your own office. No fresh light is thrown on the subject from the latest ideas developed in the world. Send for your librarian and let us see what he does.

Librarian.—Good morning, Sir.

SRR.—Glance through this file quickly. Tell me if you can help your Chairman in any way.

Librarian (after a few minutes).—I have an annotated bibliography — a recent one — on double taxation.

SRR.—Will you simply dump it on your Chairman?

Librarian.—No, Sir. If this file can be left with me for some little time, I shall be able to furnish the Chairman with a digest of only the relevant papers mentioned in the bibliography.

SRR.—Is that all?

Librarian.—I shall also pick out and send to the Chairman the full papers most relevant to this file.

After the librarian went away with that file in his hand, the Chairman said, "Honestly, I did not know Sir, that library science has grown to such a high pitch and that you have trained your librarian-students as thoroughly as you trained us — your mathematics students."

The Iaslic should ask its members to use every opportunity got by them to meet government officials as plenipotentiaries. They should convert them to the willing acceptance of documentation work and service, based on a conviction of its benefits.

54 Selling Specialist Library Service to Potential Beneficiaries

A dramatic account of all such attempts to sell the idea of documentation work and service — specialist library service — to all potential beneficiaries of it should form the bulk of the papers in the *Iaslic bulletin*, at least for a couple of decades.

55 Special Publications of Iaslic

The special publications so far published by the Iaslic are all useful. They should be continued with more of realism. In other words, they should all be illustrated by case studies — case studies capable of convincing those "on the other side of the library counter" about the value of documentation work and service.

551 *A Particularly Legitimate and Useful Kind of Publication*

While writing this book, a copy of the *Papers* of the Iaslic Conference (9) (Calcutta), published in 1972 reached my hands. Most of the papers printed in it give with notes the list of reference books published in India in diverse subjects. This is typical of the legitimate function of the Iaslic. My wish goes to the continuation of efforts of this kind. Papers of this kind can be contributed by the honorary workers constituting the Iaslic.

56 Conference and Seminar of Iaslic

Iaslic should certainly hold annually either a Conferences in our pre-independence days. A Conference often benars. For, the Conferences of many of our learned bodies — particularly those belonging to library science — have not yet escaped from the example of our political conferences in our pre-independence days. Conference often becomes a "Mela". After a splashy Opening Function, most of the time is spent in superficial talks and to visits to interesting places in the neighbourhood. I attempted to introduce the Seminar Methods (described in the *Iaslic bulletin* by C V Subba Rao) at the All India Library Conference held in Indore (1951) and in Hyderabad (1953) respectively. Then, as President I had the freedom to do so. But the sessions of each of these Conferences, using Seminar Methods, were attended only by the young authors of the papers presented to the Conference and published in advance. Many of the seniors walked away mumbling, "What is this new form of tyranny"! A description of such an allergy on the part of the seniors to serious work in a Conference will be found in Sec 65 of "Chap BM Experience with the Indian Library Association: 1933 to 1944" of my *A Librarian looks back* published as Paper

A in Vol 9, 1971 of the *Herald of library science*. On the contrary, the experience at each of the DRTC Seminars during the last nine years is of great promise. It shows the appreciation by the younger generation of the value of Seminar Method, involving concentrated continuous and serious work all through the period of the Seminar (*See* Sec H4). It has also demonstrated the willingness of the younger generation to prepare solid papers for the Seminar. It further shows the preparedness and the willingness of the younger generation to study carefully about a month in advance, the Papers submitted for consideration by the Seminar. The volume of Papers for the Iaslic Conference mentioned in Sec M551, demonstrates the happy utilisation of the Conference time of the Iaslic for truly serious work of a concerted kind.

57 Study Circles

It is quite necessary that the Iaslic should promote small study circles for developing the techniques for documentation work and service. This should be done not only in Calcutta but in many other cities in the country. The conclusions arrived at by these study circles should form the majority of the technical papers published in the *Iaslic bulletin* (*See* Sec M51 (4))

6 Iaslic-Grid Throughout the Country

Iaslic cannot realise its laudable overall objective by working mostly from its Headquarters or through annual seminars or even through its publications. As it has been already stressed, its main work should be selling the idea of specialist libraries all through the country. This can be done only personally. For this purpose, the Iaslic should establish a grid of its branches in all the localities of the country rich in industrial and commercial enterprises and research organisations. The members of these branches should contact the potential beneficiaries of specialist libraries in their respective areas. The members should demonstrate to each potential consumer the value of documentation work and service. (For an example *See* Sec M533). They should also collect data from the users of specialist libraries about the help received from them. The data should also cover the opinion of the users about the inadequacy and improvement, if any, in the service received by them. They should form the realistic case studies for inclusion in the *Iaslic bulletin*. This will soon set up a chain reaction towards the wide acceptance of specialist library service throughout the country. Incidentally, the establishment of such branches will go a long way in bringing about the realisation of the wish mentioned in the succeeding section about the "Band of Documentation Missionaries".

7 Band of Documentation Missionaries

My imagination makes me feel that the Iaslic should raise a band of documentation missionaries. They should be persons with rich experience in documentation work and service in specialist libraries. They should be persons who love documentation work and service. They should be persons totally convinced about the need for documentation work and service in our fast developing country. This is necessary to enable it to reach self-sufficiency and become a peer among other nations in as short a time as possible. They should be persons finding joy (*Pramōda*), delight (*Ānanda*), and full self-satisfaction (*Ātma-tripti*) in helping the research work in our country — pure as well as applied. They should be persons who, by the Grace of Mahasaraswati, "Abhor carelessness and negligence and indolence, all scamped and hasty and shuffling work, leaving off things undone or half done".

INDEX

Prepared by P Jayarajan, *Research Assistant to National Research Professor in Library Science, DRTC, Bangalore 3.*

Note.—

1 The index number in each entry is the number of the Chapter or Section in which the item occurs in the book.

2 The first letter — lower-case or capital — in the index number denotes the Chapter.

3 The Indo-Arabic numeral, following the first letter, denotes the Section.

Example: C7 = Section 7 in Chapter C

Contractions used: *def* = defined at
irt = in relation to
qirt = quoted in relation to
r by = referred by
rirt = referred in relation to